Registration Document 2013
Air France-KLM

including the annual financial report

This Registration Document is an unofficial translation of the French Document de Référence, which was filed with the French Autorité des Marchés Financiers on Tuesday April 8, 2014, pursuant to article 212-13 of the AMF General Regulations. This unofficial translation has been prepared by Air France-KLM for the information and convenience of English-speaking readers and has not been reviewed or registered with the AMF. No assurances are given as to the accuracy or completeness of this translation, nor any responsibility assumed for any misstatement or omission that may be contained therein. The French Document de Référence may be used for the purposes of a financial transaction if supplemented with an offering memorandum approved by the AMF. In the event of any ambiguity or discrepancy between this unofficial translation and the French Document de Référence, the French version shall prevail.

This page has been intentionally left blank

Contents

5.5 Consolidated financial statements

5.6 Notes to the consolidated financial statements

5.5 Consolidated financial statements

Financial year ended December 31, 2013

5.5.1 Consolidated income statement

Period from January 1 to December 31 *(In € million)*	Notes	2013	2012 Pro forma*
Sales	6	**25,520**	**25,423**
Other revenues		10	16
Revenues		**25,530**	**25,439**
External expenses	7	(15,997)	(16,272)
Salaries and related costs	8	(7,482)	(7,662)
Taxes other than income taxes		(186)	(184)
Amortization	9	(1,566)	(1,576)
Depreciation and provisions	9	(159)	(154)
Other income and expenses	10	(10)	73
Income from current operations		**130**	**(336)**
Sales of aircraft equipment	11	(12)	8
Other non-current income and expenses	11	(345)	(403)
Income from operating activities		**(227)**	**(731)**
Cost of financial debt		(481)	(436)
Income from cash and cash equivalents		77	83
Net cost of financial debt	12	**(404)**	**(353)**
Other financial income and expenses	12	103	144
Income before tax		**(528)**	**(940)**
Income taxes	13	(957)	(17)
Net income of consolidated companies		**(1,485)**	**(957)**
Share of profits (losses) of associates	22	(211)	(66)
Net income from continuing operations		**(1,696)**	**(1,023)**
Net income from discontinued operations	14	(122)	(197)
Net income for the period		**(1,818)**	**(1,220)**
Equity holders of Air France-KLM		**(1,827)**	**(1,225)**
Non controlling interests		9	5
Earnings per share – Equity holders of Air France-KLM *(in euros)*			
♦ Basic and diluted	16.1	(6.17)	(4.14)
Net income from continuing operations - Equity holders of Air France-KLM *(in euros)*			
♦ Basic and diluted	16.1	(5.76)	(3.47)
Net income from discontinued operations - Equity holders of Air France-KLM *(in euros)*			
♦ Basic and diluted	16.1	(0.41)	(0.67)

* *See Note 2 "Restatement of the 2012 financial statements" in notes to the consolidated financial statements.*

The accompanying notes are an integral part of these consolidated financial statements.

5.5.2 Consolidated statement of recognized income and expenses

(In € million)	December 31, 2013	December 31, 2012 Pro forma*
Net income for the period	*(1,818)*	*(1,220)*
Fair value adjustment on available-for-sale securities		
◆ Change in fair value recognized directly in other comprehensive income	420	269
◆ Change in fair value transferred to profit or loss	-	(97)
Fair value hedges		
Effective portion of changes in fair value hedge recognized directly in other comprehensive income	(101)	-
Cash flow hedges		
◆ Effective portion of changes in fair value hedge recognized directly in other comprehensive income	213	124
◆ Change in fair value transferred to profit or loss	(120)	(251)
Currency translation adjustment	(2)	-
Deferred tax on items of comprehensive income that will be reclassified to profit or loss	(10)	30
Items of the recognized income and expenses of equity shares, net of tax	(4)	(7)
Total of other comprehensive income that will be reclassified to profit or loss	*396*	*68*
Remeasurements of defined benefit pension plans	26	(313)
Deferred tax on items of comprehensive income that will not be reclassified to profit or loss	(18)	95
Remeasurements of defined benefit pension plans of equity shares, net of tax	(1)	(2)
Total of other comprehensive income that will not be reclassified to profit or loss	*7*	*(220)*
Total of other comprehensive income, after tax	*403*	*(152)*
Recognized income and expenses	*(1,415)*	*(1,372)*
◆ *Equity holders of Air France-KLM*	*(1,423)*	*(1,376)*
◆ Non-controlling interests	8	4

* See Note 2 "Restatement of the 2012 financial statements" in notes to the consolidated financial statements.

The accompanying notes are an integral part of these consolidated financial statements.

5.5.3 Consolidated balance sheet

Assets (In € million)	Notes	December 31, 2013	December 31, 2012 Pro forma*	January 1, 2012 Pro forma*
Goodwill	17	237	252	426
Intangible assets	18	896	842	774
Flight equipment	20	9,391	10,048	10,689
Other property, plant and equipment	20	1,819	1,932	2,055
Investments in equity associates	22	177	381	422
Pension assets	23	2,454	2,477	2,336
Other financial assets**	24	1,963	1,665	2,015
Deferred tax assets	13.4	436	1,392	1,322
Other non-current assets	27	113	152	168
Total non-current assets		*17,486*	*19,141*	*20,207*
Assets held for sale	15	91	7	10
Other short-term financial assets**	24	1,031	933	751
Inventories	25	511	521	585
Trade accounts receivables	26	1,775	1,859	1,774
Income tax receivables		23	11	10
Other current assets	27	822	828	995
Cash and cash equivalents	28	3,684	3,420	2,283
Total current assets		*7,937*	*7,579*	*6,408*
Total assets		**25,423**	**26,720**	**26,615**

* See Note 2 "Restatement of the 2012 financial statements" in notes to the consolidated financial statements.
** Including:

(In € million)	December 31, 2013	December 31, 2012 Pro forma*	January 1, 2012 Pro forma*
Deposits related to financial debts	780	806	656
Marketable securities (including cash secured)	951	956	987

The accompanying notes are an integral part of these consolidated financial statements.

Liabilities and equity *(In € million)*	Notes	December 31, 2013	December 31, 2012 Pro forma*	January 1, 2012 Pro forma*
Issued capital	29.1	300	300	300
Additional paid-in capital	29.2	2,971	2,971	2,971
Treasury shares	29.3	(85)	(85)	(89)
Reserves and retained earnings	29.4	(944)	403	1,775
Equity attributable to equity holders of Air France-KLM		*2,242*	*3,589*	*4,957*
Non-controlling interests		48	48	47
Total equity		*2,290*	*3,637*	*5,004*
Provisions and retirement benefits	31	3,102	3,158	2,692
Long-term debt	32	8,596	9,565	9,228
Deferred tax liabilities	13.4	178	149	223
Other non-current liabilities	33	397	384	321
Total non-current liabilities		*12,273*	*13,256*	*12,464*
Liabilities relating to assets held for sale	15	58	-	-
Provisions	31	670	555	156
Current portion of long-term debt	32	2,137	1,434	1,174
Trade accounts payables		2,369	2,219	2,599
Deferred revenue on ticket sales		2,371	2,115	1,885
Frequent flyer programs		755	770	784
Current tax liabilities		2	3	6
Other current liabilities	33	2,332	2,474	2,386
Bank overdrafts	28	166	257	157
Total current liabilities		*10,860*	*9,827*	*9,147*
Total liabilities		**23,133**	**23,083**	**21,611**
Total liabilities and equity		**25,423**	**26,720**	**26,615**

* See Note 2 "Restatement of the 2012 financial statements" in notes to the consolidated financial statements.

The accompanying notes are an integral part of these consolidated financial statements.

5.5.4 Consolidated statement of changes in stockholders' equity

(In € million)	Number of shares	Issued capital	Additional paid-in capital	Treasury shares	Reserves and retained earnings	Equity attributable to holders of Air France-KLM	Non controlling interests	Total equity
January 1, 2012	300,219,278	300	2,971	(89)	2,858	6,040	54	6,094
First application of IAS 19 Revised " Employee Benefits" (Note 2)	-	-	-	-	(1,083)	(1,083)	(7)	(1,090)
January 1, 2012 (Pro forma) *	300,219,278	300	2,971	(89)	1,775	4,957	47	5,004
Fair value adjustment on available for sale securities	-	-	-	-	168	168	-	168
Gain/ (loss) on cash flow hedges	-	-	-	-	(100)	(100)	-	(100)
Remeasurements of defined benefit pension plans	-	-	-	-	(219)	(219)	(1)	(220)
Other comprehensive income	-	-	-	-	(151)	(151)	(1)	(152)
Net income for the year	-	-	-	-	(1,225)	(1,225)	5	(1,220)
Total of income and expenses recognized	-	-	-	-	(1,376)	(1,376)	4	(1,372)
Stock based compensation (ESA) and stock option	-	-	-	-	3	3	-	3
Dividends paid	-	-	-	-	-	-	(2)	(2)
Treasury shares	-	-	-	4	-	4	-	4
Change in consolidation scope	-	-	-	-	1	1	(1)	-
December 31, 2012 (Pro forma) *	300,219,278	300	2,971	(85)	403	3,589	48	3,637
Fair value adjustment on available for sale securities	-	-	-	-	402	402	-	402
Gain / (loss) on cash flow hedges	-	-	-	-	62	62	-	62
Gain /(loss) on fair value hedges	-	-	-	-	(66)	(66)	-	(66)
Remeasurements of defined benefit pension plans	-	-	-	-	8	8	(1)	7
Currency translation adjustment	-	-	-	-	(2)	(2)	-	(2)
Other comprehensive income	-	-	-	-	404	404	(1)	403
Net income for the year	-	-	-	-	(1,827)	(1,827)	9	(1,818)
Total of income and expenses recognized	-	-	-	-	(1,423)	(1,423)	8	(1,415)
Stock based compensation (ESA) and stock option	-	-	-	-	3	3	-	3
OCEANE	-	-	-	-	70	70	-	70
Treasury shares	-	-	-	-	(1)	(1)	-	(1)
Dividends paid	-	-	-	-	-	-	(4)	(4)
Change in consolidation scope	-	-	-	-	4	4	(4)	-
December 31, 2013	300,219,278	300	2,971	(85)	(944)	2,242	48	2,290

* See Note 2 "Restatement of the 2012 financial statements" in notes to the consolidated financial statements.

The accompanying notes are an integral part of these consolidated financial statements.

5.5.5 Consolidated statements of cash flows

(In € million) **Period from January 1 to December 31**	**Notes**	**2013**	**2012** **Pro forma***
Net income from continuing operations		(1,696)	(1,023)
Net income from discontinued operations	14	(122)	(197)
Amortization, depreciation and operating provisions	9	1,735	1,748
Financial provisions	12	28	(15)
Gain on disposals of tangible and intangible assets		12	(24)
Loss / (gain) on disposals of subsidiaries and associates	11	(6)	(97)
Derivatives – non monetary result		(61)	(86)
Unrealized foreign exchange gains and losses, net		(114)	(94)
Share of (profits) losses of associates	22	211	66
Deferred taxes	13	916	(21)
Impairment	39.1	79	173
Other non-monetary	39.1	127	372
Subtotal		*1,109*	*802*
Of which discontinued operations		*(19)*	*(5)*
(Increase) / decrease in inventories		1	65
(Increase) / decrease in trade receivables		59	(142)
Increase / (decrease) in trade payables		55	(299)
Change in other receivables and payables		228	416
Change in working capital from discontinued operations		27	9
Net cash flow from operating activities		*1,479*	*851*
Acquisition of subsidiaries, of shares in non-controlled entities	39.2	(27)	(39)
Purchase of property, plant and equipment and intangible assets	21	(1,186)	(1,465)
Loss of subsidiaries, of disposal of shares in non-controlled entities	11	27	467
Proceeds on disposal of property, plant and equipment and intangible assets		245	742
Dividends received		17	24
Decrease (increase) in net investments, between 3 months and 1 year		5	30
Net cash flow used in investing activities of discontinued operations		(5)	(4)
Net cash flow used in investing activities		*(924)*	*(245)*

(In € million) Period from January 1 to December 31	Notes	2013	2012 Pro forma*
Increase in capital		6	-
Disposal of subsidiaries without loss of control, of owned shares	39.3	-	7
Issuance of debt		1,887	1,780
Repayment on debt		(1,480)	(847)
Payment of debt resulting from finance lease liabilities		(588)	(514)
New loans		(136)	(90)
Repayment on loans		157	100
Dividends paid		(4)	(2)
Net cash flow from financing activities		*(158)*	*434*
Effect of exchange rate on cash and cash equivalents and bank overdrafts		(36)	(1)
Effect of exchange rate on cash and cash equivalents and bank overdrafts of discontinued operations		1	(2)
Change in cash and cash equivalents and bank overdrafts		*362*	*1,037*
Cash and cash equivalents and bank overdrafts at beginning of period	28	3,160	2,121
Cash and cash equivalents and bank overdrafts at end of period	28	3,518	3,160
Change in cash of discontinued operations		4	(2)
Income tax (paid) / reimbursed (flow included in operating activities)		(48)	(45)
Interest paid (flow included in operating activities)		(403)	(414)
Interest received (flow included in operating activities)		41	35

* See Note 2 "Restatement of the 2012 financial statements" in notes to the consolidated financial statements.

The accompanying notes are an integral part of these consolidated financial statements.

5.6 Notes to the consolidated financial statements

Note 1 Business description

As used herein, the term "Air France-KLM" refers to Air France-KLM SA, a limited liability company organized under French law.

The term "Group" is represented by the economic definition of Air France-KLM and its subsidiaries. The Group is headquartered in France and is one of the largest airlines in the world. The Group's core business is passenger transportation. The Group's activities also include cargo, aeronautics maintenance and other air-transport-related activities including, principally, catering and charter services.

The limited company Air France-KLM, domiciled at 2 rue Robert Esnault-Pelterie 75007 Paris, France, is the parent company of the Air France-KLM Group. Air France-KLM is listed for trading in Paris (Euronext) and Amsterdam (Euronext).

The presentation currency used in the Group's financial statements is the euro, which is also Air France-KLM's functional currency.

Note 2 Restatements of the 2012 financial statements

2.1 Application of IAS 19 Revised

Since January 1, 2013, the IAS 19 Revised "Employee Benefits" standard, published by the IASB in June 2011, has been applicable. The main changes for the Group are as follows:

+ the option previously used by the Group, allowing the amortization of actuarial differences with the «corridor» method, has been deleted. Actuarial gains and losses are now recognized immediately in other comprehensive income;

The impacts of the revision in the standard are summarized below:

+ non-vested past service costs, previously amortized, are now fully recognized in the income statement;
+ the return on assets, previously determined from an expected rate of return, is now assessed on the basis of the discount rate used to value the benefit obligations.

The consolidated financial statements as of December 31, 2012 have been restated to facilitate comparison. The restated balance sheet as of January 1, 2012 is also presented.

➤ Impacts on the consolidated income statement

(In € million)	December 31, 2012
Salaries and related costs	(53)
Other non-current income and expenses	13
Income taxes	7
Net income for the period	*(33)*
♦ *Equity holders of Air France-KLM*	(33)
♦ *Non-controlling interests*	-
Earnings per share – Equity holders of Air France-KLM (in euros)	
♦ *Basic*	*(0.11)*
♦ *Diluted*	*(0.11)*

> **Impacts on the consolidated statement of recognized income and expenses**

(In € million)	December 31, 2012
Net income for the period	*(33)*
Remeasurements of defined benefit pension plans	(313)
Items of the recognized income and expenses of equity shares	(2)
Tax on items of other comprehensive income that will not be reclassified to profit or loss	95
Recognized income and expenses	*(253)*
◆ *Equity holders of Air France-KLM*	*(252)*
◆ *Non-controlling interests*	*(1)*

> **Impacts on the consolidated balance sheet**

(In € million)	January 1, 2012	December 31, 2012
Investments in equity associates	-	(2)
Pension assets	(881)	(993)
Deferred tax assets	179	241
Provisions and retirement benefits	631	871
Deferred tax liabilities	(243)	(282)
Net impacts on equity	(1,090)	(1,343)
◆ *Equity holders of Air France-KLM*	*(1,083)*	*(1,335)*
◆ *Non-controlling interests*	*(7)*	*(8)*

2.2 Presentation of the CityJet Group's financial statements as a discontinued operation

On December 20, 2013, Air France received a firm offer from Intro Aviation GmbH to purchase its subsidiaries CityJet and VLM. The employee representative bodies of the relevant companies need to be informed and consulted to enable the disposal to be finalized. The CityJet Group, who has always dealed on its own trademark, comprises the only airlines in the Group that operate:

◆ outside the short/medium-haul scope defined by the Transform 2015 plan;

◆ mainly on the basis of London City which appears non-complementary to the Group activities;

◆ with few operational links or "businesses" with the rest of the company (maintenance, information systems, etc.).

This unit represents a clearly identifiable component, with limited links to the rest of the Group but nevertheless significant in term of business.

As result, the planned disposal justifies the discontinued operations treatment, as defined in the standard IFRS 5. The detail on the net income from discontinued operations is given in Note 14.

Note 3 Significant events

3.1 Change in the scope of consolidation

Within the framework of the Transform 2015 project, the Air France Group decided to regroup its French regional activities Britair, Régional and Airlinair within a holding company known as *HOP! (see Note 5)*, and, during the third quarter, announced the deployment of additional measures to reduce costs concerning the restructuring plan launched in 2012. Based on the measures presented to the different bodies officially representing the Air France Group, the Group has made, to date, its best estimate of the new costs involved and has booked an additional provision for restructuring *(see Note 11)*.

On March 28, 2013, Air France-KLM issued 53,398,058 bonds convertible and/or exchangeable for new or existing Air France-KLM shares (OCEANE) maturing on February 15, 2023 for an amount of €550 million *(see Note 32)*.

On June 19, 2013, the Group finalized the firm order for 25 Airbus A350s, in accordance with the letter of intention signed on May 27, 2013.

Following its decision not to participate in the Alitalia capital increase of October 2013, and after conversion into equity of the €23.8 million shareholder loan subscribed in February 25, 2013, the Air France-KLM Group saw its shareholding in Alitalia decrease from 25% to 7.08% *(see Notes 5, 11, 22 and 24)*.

3.2 Subsequent events

There has been no significant event since the closing of the financial year.

Note 4 Rules and accounting principles

4.1 Accounting principles

4.1.1 Accounting principles used for consolidated financial statements

Pursuant to the European Regulation 1606/2002, July 19, 2002, the consolidated financial statements as of December 31, 2013 have been prepared in accordance with International Financial Reporting Standards ("IFRS") as adopted by the European Commission ("EU") and applicable on the date these consolidated financial statements were established.

IFRS as adopted by the EU differ in certain respects from IFRS as published by the International Accounting Standards Board ("IASB"). The Group has, however, determined that the financial information for the periods presented would not differ substantially if the Group had applied IFRS as published by the IASB.

The consolidated financial statements were approved by the Board of Directors on February 19, 2014.

4.1.2 Change in accounting principles

❚ *IFRS standards, amendments and IFRIC interpretations (IFRS Interpretation Committee) applicable on a mandatory basis to the 2013 financial statements*

The texts whose application became mandatory during the accounting period ended December 31, 2013 are the following:

✦ standard IFRS 13 " Fair Value Measurement";
✦ amendment to IFRS 7 "Disclosures – Offsetting Financial assets and Financial liabilities";
✦ amendment to IAS 1 on presentation of other comprehensive income;
✦ standard IAS 19 Revised" Employee Benefit";
✦ annual improvements to IFRS 2009-11.

The impacts of IAS 19 Revised on the Group's consolidated financial statements are detailed in Note 2 "Restatements of the 2012 financial statements". The other standards and amendments mentioned above did not have any significant impact on the Group's consolidated financial statements as of December 31, 2013.

The other texts whose application became mandatory during the year ended December 31, 2013 had no impact on the Group's consolidated financial statements.

❚ *IFRS standards, amendments and IFRIC interpretations which are not applicable on a mandatory basis to the 2013 financial statements*

✦ Standard IFRS 10 "Consolidated Financial Statements" which will replace IAS 27 "Consolidated and Separate Financial Statements" for the part concerning the consolidated financial statements and also the SIC 12 interpretation "Consolidation – Special Purpose Entities" (applicable on a mandatory basis from fiscal years starting on January 1, 2014).
✦ Standard IFRS 11 "Joint Arrangements" which will replace IAS 31 "Interests in Joint Ventures" and also the SIC 13 interpretation "Jointly Controlled Entities – Non-Monetary Contributions by Venturers (applicable on a mandatory basis from fiscal years starting on January 1, 2014).
✦ Standard IFRS 12 "Disclosure on Interests in Other Entities (applicable on a mandatory basis from fiscal years starting on January 1, 2014).
✦ Standard IAS 28 (2011) "Investments in Associates (applicable on a mandatory basis from fiscal years starting on January 1, 2014).
✦ Amendment to IAS 32 "Presentation - Offsetting Financial assets and Financial liabilities (applicable on a mandatory basis from fiscal years starting on January 1, 2014).

The application of IFRS 10 and IFRS 11 is currently being considered. Nevertheless, the Group does not expect any significant changes in its consolidation scope.

▮ *IFRS standards and IFRIC interpretations which are applicable on a mandatory basis to the 2014 financial statements*

◆ Amendment to IAS 36 "Recoverable Amount Disclosures for Non Financial Assets".

◆ Amendment to IAS 39 "Novation of Derivatives and Continuation of Hedge Accounting".

▮ *Other texts potentially applicable to the Group, published by the IASB but not yet adopted by the European Union, are described below*

◆ Interpretation IFRIC 21 "Levies" applicable from January 1, 2014.

◆ Standard IFRS 9 "Financial instruments - Classification and measurement of financial assets and liabilities", applicable not earlier than January 2017 because the IASB has postponed the initial effective date from January 2015 to another as-yet-unset date.

4.2 Use of estimates

The preparation of the consolidated financial statements in conformity with IFRS requires management to make estimates and use assumptions that affect the reported amounts of assets and liabilities and the disclosures of contingent assets and liabilities at the date of the consolidated financial statements and the reported amounts of revenues and expenses. The main estimates are described in the following notes:

◆ Note 4.6 – Revenue recognition related to deferred revenue on ticket sales;

◆ Notes 4.13 and 4.12 – Tangible and intangible assets;

◆ Note 4.10 – Financial instruments;

◆ Note 4.22 – Deferred taxes;

◆ Note 4.7 – "Flying Blue" frequent flyer program;

◆ Notes 4.17, 4.18 and 4.19 – Provisions (including employee benefits).

The Group's management makes these estimates and assessments continuously on the basis of its past experience and various other factors considered to be reasonable.

The consolidated financial statements for the financial year have thus been established taking into account the economic and financial crisis unfolding since 2008 and on the basis of financial parameters available at the closing date. The immediate effects of the crisis have been taken into account, in particular the valuation of current assets and liabilities. Concerning the longer-term assets, i.e. the non-current assets, the assumptions are based on limited growth.

The future results could differ from these estimates depending on changes in the assumptions used or different conditions.

4.3 Consolidation principles

4.3.1 Subsidiaries

Companies over which the Group exercises control are fully consolidated. Control is defined as the power to govern the financial and operating policies of an entity so as to obtain benefits from its activities. The financial statements of subsidiaries are included in the consolidated financial statements from the date that control begins until the date this control ceases.

Non-controlling interests are presented within equity and on the income statement separately from Group stockholders' equity and the Group's net income, under the line "non-controlling interests".

The effects of a buyout of non-controlling interests in a subsidiary already controlled by the Group and divestment of a percentage interest without loss of control are recognized in equity.

In a partial disposal resulting in loss of control, the retained equity interest is remeasured at fair value at the date of loss of control. The gain or loss on the disposal will include the effect of this remeasurement and the gain or loss on the sale of the equity interest, including all the items initially recognized in equity and reclassified to profit and loss.

4.3.2 Interest in associates and joint-ventures

Companies in which the Group has the ability to exercise significant influence on financial and operating policy decisions are accounted for using the equity method; the ability to exercise significant influence is presumed to exist when the Group holds more than 20% of the voting rights.

In addition, companies in which the Group exercises joint control according to a contractual agreement are accounted for using the equity method.

The consolidated financial statements include the Group's share of the total recognized global result of associates and joint-ventures from the date the ability to exercise significant influence begins to the date it ceases, adjusted for any impairment loss.

The Group's share of losses of an associate that exceed the value of the Group's interest and net investment (long-term receivables for which no reimbursement is scheduled or likely) in this entity are not accounted for, unless:

◆ the Group has incurred contractual obligations; or

◆ the Group has made payments on behalf of the associate.

Any surplus of the investment cost over the Group's share in the fair value of the identifiable assets, liabilities and contingent liabilities of the associate company on the date of acquisition is accounted for as goodwill and included in the book value of the investment accounted for using the equity method.

The investments in which the Group has ceased to exercise significant influence or joint control are no longer accounted for by the equity method and are valued at their fair value on the date of loss of significant influence or joint control.

4.3.3 Intra-group operations

All intra-group balances and transactions, including income, expenses and dividends are fully eliminated. Profits and losses resulting from intra-group transactions that are recognized in assets are also eliminated.

Gains and losses realized on internal sales with associates and jointly-controlled entities are eliminated, to the extent of the Group's interest in the entity, providing there is no impairment.

4.4 Translation of foreign companies' financial statements and transactions in foreign currencies

4.4.1 Translation of foreign companies' financial statements

The financial statements of foreign subsidiaries are translated into euros on the following basis:

+ except for the equity for which historical prices are applied, balance sheet items are converted on the basis of the foreign currency exchange rates in effect at the closing date;
+ the income statement and the statement of cash flows are converted on the basis of the average foreign currency exchange rates for the period;
+ the resulting foreign currency exchange adjustment is recorded in the «Translation adjustments» item included within equity.

Goodwill is expressed in the functional currency of the entity acquired and is converted into euros using the foreign exchange rate in effect at the closing date.

4.4.2 Translation of foreign currency transactions

Foreign currency transactions are translated using the exchange rate prevailing on the date of the transaction.

Monetary assets and liabilities denominated in foreign currencies are translated at the rate in effect at the closing date or at the rate of the related hedge if any.

Non-monetary assets and liabilities denominated in foreign currencies assessed on an historical cost basis are translated using the rate in effect at the transaction date or using the hedged rate where necessary (see 4.13.2).

The corresponding exchange rate differences are recorded in the Group's consolidated income statement. Changes in fair value of the hedging instruments are recorded using the accounting treatment described in Note 4.10 "Financial instruments, valuation of financial assets and liabilities".

4.5 Business combinations

4.5.1 Business combinations completed on or after April 1, 2010

Business combinations completed on or after April 1, 2010 are accounted for using the purchase method in accordance with IFRS 3

(2008) "Business combinations". In accordance with this standard, all assets and liabilities assumed are measured at fair value at the acquisition date. The time period for adjustments to goodwill/negative goodwill is limited to 12 months from the date of acquisition, except for non-current assets classified as assets held for sale which are measured at fair value less costs to sell.

Goodwill corresponding, at the acquisition date, to the aggregate of the consideration transferred and the amount of any non-controlling interest in the acquiree minus the net amounts (usually at fair value) of the identifiable assets acquired and the liabilities assumed at the acquisition date, is subject to annual impairment tests or more frequently if events or changes in circumstances indicate that goodwill might be impaired.

Costs other than those related to the issuance of debt or equity securities are recognized immediately as an expense when incurred.

For each acquisition, the Group has the option of using the "full" goodwill method, where goodwill is calculated by taking into account the fair value of non-controlling interests at the acquisition date rather than their proportionate interest in the fair value of the assets and liabilities of the acquiree.

Should the fair value of identifiable assets acquired and liabilities assumed exceed the consideration transferred, the resulting negative goodwill is recognized immediately in the income statement.

Contingent considerations or earn-outs are recorded in equity if contingent payment is settled by delivery of a fixed number of the acquirer's equity instruments (according to IAS 32). In all other cases, they are recognized in liabilities related to business combinations. Contingent payments or earn-outs are measured at fair value at the acquisition date. This initial measurement is subsequently adjusted through goodwill only when additional information is obtained after the acquisition date about facts and circumstances that existed at that date. Such adjustments are made only during the 12-month measurement period that follows the acquisition date. Any other subsequent adjustments which do not meet these criteria are recorded as receivables or payables through the income statement.

In a step acquisition, the previously-held equity interest in the acquiree is remeasured at its acquisition-date fair value. The difference between the fair value and the net book value must be accounted in profit or loss as well as elements previously recognized in other comprehensive income.

4.5.2 Business combination carried out before April 1, 2010

Business combinations carried out before April 1, 2010 are accounted for using the purchase method in accordance with IFRS 3 (2004) "Business combinations". In accordance with this standard, all assets, liabilities assumed and contingent liabilities are measured at fair value at the acquisition date. The time period for adjustments to goodwill/negative goodwill is limited to 12 months from the date of acquisition.

Assets meeting the criteria of IFRS 5 "Non-current assets held for sale and discontinued operations", as described in Note 4.23, are recorded at the lower of their net book value and their fair value less costs to sell.

Goodwill arising from the difference between the acquisition cost, which includes the potential equity instruments issued by the Group to gain control over the acquired entity and other costs potentially dedicated to the business combination, and the Group's interest in the fair value of the identifiable assets and liabilities acquired, is subject to annual impairment tests or more frequently if events or changes in circumstances indicate that goodwill might be impaired.

Should the fair value of identifiable assets acquired and liabilities assumed exceed the cost of acquisition, the resulting negative goodwill is recognized immediately in the income statement.

4.6   Sales

Sales related to air transportation operations are recognized when the transportation service is provided, net of any discounts granted. Transportation service is also the trigger for the recognition of external expenses, such as the commissions paid to agents.

Both passenger and cargo tickets are consequently recorded as "Deferred revenue on ticket sales".

Sales relating to the value of tickets that have been issued, but never be used, are recognized as revenues at issuance. The amounts recognized are based on a statistical analysis, which is regularly updated.

Sales on third-party maintenance contracts are recorded on the basis of completion method.

4.7   Loyalty programs

The two sub-groups Air France and KLM have a common frequent flyer program *Flying Blue*. This program enables members to acquire "miles" as they fly with airlines partners or transactions with non airline partners (credit cards, hotels, car rental agencies). These miles entitle members to a variety of benefits such as free flights with the two companies or other free services with non flying partners.

In accordance with IFRIC 13 "Loyalty programs", these "miles" are considered as distinct elements from a sale with multiple elements and one part of the price of the initial sale of the airfare is allocated to these "miles" and deferred until the Group's commitments relating to these "miles" have been met. The deferred amount due in relation to the acquisition of miles by members is estimated:

+ according to the fair value of the "miles", defined as the amount at which the benefits can be sold separately;
+ after taking into account the redemption rate, corresponding to the probability that the miles will be used by members, using a statistical method.

With regards to the invoicing of other partners in the program, the margins realized on sales of "miles" by the sub-groups Air France and KLM to other partners are recorded immediately in the income statement.

4.8   Distinction between income from current operations and income from operating activities

The Group considers it is relevant to the understanding of its financial performance to present in the income statement a subtotal within the income from operating activities. This subtotal, entitled "Income from current operations", excludes unusual elements that do not have predictive value due to their nature, frequency and/or materiality, as defined in the recommendation no. 2009-R.03 from the National Accounting Council.

Such elements are as follows:

+ sales of aircraft equipment and disposals of other assets;
+ income from the disposal of subsidiaries and affiliates;
+ restructuring costs when they are significant;
+ significant and infrequent elements such as the recognition of badwill in the income statement, recording an impairment loss on goodwill and significant provisions for litigation.

4.9   Earnings per share

Earnings per share are calculated by dividing net income attributable to the equity holders of Air France-KLM by the average number of shares outstanding during the period. The average number of shares outstanding does not include treasury shares.

Diluted earnings per share are calculated by dividing the net income attributable to the equity holders of Air France-KLM adjusted for the effects of dilutive instrument exercise, by the average number of shares outstanding during the period, adjusted for the effect of all potentially-dilutive ordinary shares.

4.10   Financial instruments, valuation of financial assets and liabilities

4.10.1 Valuation of trade receivables and non-current financial assets

Trade receivables, loans and other non-current financial assets are considered to be assets issued by the Group and are recorded at fair value then, subsequently, using the amortized cost method less impairment losses, if any. The purchases and sales of financial assets are accounted for as of the transaction date.

4.10.2 Investments in equity securities

Investments in equity securities qualifying as assets available for sale are stated at fair value in the Group's balance sheet. For publicly-traded securities, the fair value is considered to be the market price at the closing date. For other securities, if the fair value cannot be reliably estimated, the Group uses the exception of accounting at costs (i.e acquisition cost less impairment, if any).

Potential gains and losses, except for impairment charges, are recorded in a specific component of other comprehensive income "Derivatives and available for sale securities reserves". If there is an indication of impairment of the financial asset, the amount of the loss resulting from the impairment test is recorded in the income statement for the period.

4.10.3 Derivative financial instruments

The Group uses various derivative financial instruments to hedge its exposure to the risks incurred on shares, exchange rates, changes in interest rates or fuel prices.

Forward currency contracts and options are used to cover exposure to exchange rates. For firm commitments, the unrealized gains and losses on these financial instruments are included in the carrying value of the hedged asset or liability.

The Group also uses rate swaps to manage its exposure to interest rate risk. Most of the swaps traded convert floating-rate debt to fixed-rate debt.

Finally, exposure to the fuel risk is hedged by swaps or options on jet fuel, diesel or Brent.

Most of these derivatives are classified as hedging instruments if the derivative is eligible as a hedging instrument and if the hedging contracts are documented as required by IAS 39 "Financial instruments: recognition and measurement".

These derivative instruments are recorded on the Group's consolidated balance sheet at their fair value taken into account the market value of the credit risk of the Group (DVA) and the credit risk of the counterpart (CVA). The calculation of credit risk follows a common model based on default probabilities from CDS counterparts.

The method of accounting for changes in fair value depends on the classification of the derivative instruments. There are three classifications:

+ *derivatives classified as fair value hedge*: changes in the derivative fair value are recorded through the income statement and offset within the limit of its effective portion against the changes in the fair value of the underlying item (assets, liability or firm commitment), which are also recognized as earnings;
+ *derivatives classified as cash flow hedge*: the changes in fair value are recorded in other comprehensive income for the effective portion and are reclassified as income when the hedged element affects earnings. The ineffective portion is recorded as financial income or losses;
+ *derivatives classified as trading*: changes in the derivative fair value are recorded as financial income or losses.

4.10.4 Convertible bonds

Convertible bonds are financial instruments comprising two components: a bond component recorded as debt and a stock component recorded in equity. The bond component is equal to the discounted value of all coupons due for the bond at the rate of a simple bond that would have been issued at the same time as the convertible bond. The value of the stock component recorded in the Group's equity is calculated by the difference between such value and the bond's nominal value at issue. The difference between the financial expense recorded and the amounts effectively paid out is added, at each closing date, to the amount of the debt component so that, at maturity, the amount to be repaid if there is no conversion equals the redemption price.

4.10.5 Financial assets, cash and cash equivalents

▮ *Financial assets at fair value through profit and loss*

Financial assets include financial assets at fair value through profit and loss (French mutual funds such as SICAVs and FCPs, certificates, etc.) that the Group intends to sell in the near term to realize a capital gain, or that are part of a portfolio of identified financial instruments managed collectively and for which there is evidence of a practice of short-term profit taking. They are classified in the balance sheet as current financial assets. Furthermore, the Group opted not to designate any assets at fair value through the income statement.

▮ *Cash and cash equivalents*

Cash and cash equivalents are short-term, highly liquid investments that are readily convertible to known amounts of cash and which are subject to an insignificant risk of change in value.

4.10.6 Long-term debt

Long-term debt is recognized initially at fair value. Subsequent to the initial measurement, long-term debt is recorded at amortized cost calculated using the effective interest rate. Under this principle, any redemption and issue premiums are recorded as debt in the balance sheet and amortized as financial income or expense over the life of the loans.

In addition, long-term debt documented in the context of fair value hedging relationships is revalued at the fair value for the risk hedged, i.e. the risk related to the fluctuation in interest rates. Changes in fair value of the hedged debt are recorded symmetrically in the income statement for the period with the change in fair value of the hedging swaps.

4.10.7 Fair value hierarchy

The table presenting a breakdown of financial assets and liabilities categorized by value *(see Note 34.4)* meets the amended requirements of IFRS 7 "Financial instruments: Disclosures". The fair values are classified using a scale which reflects the nature of the market data used to make the valuations.

This scale has three levels of fair value.

+ **Level 1**: fair value calculated from the exchange rate/price quoted on the active market for identical instruments;
+ **Level 2**: fair value calculated from valuation methods based on observable data such as the prices of similar assets and liabilities or scopes quoted on the active market;
+ **Level 3**: fair value calculated from valuation methods which rely completely or in part on non-observable data such as prices on an inactive market or the valuation on a multiples basis for non-quoted securities.

4.11 Goodwill

Goodwill corresponds, at the acquisition date, to the aggregation of the consideration transferred and the amount of any non-controlling interest in the acquiree minus the net amounts (usually at fair value) of the identifiable amounts acquired and the liabilities assumed at the acquisition-date.

For acquisitions prior to April 1, 2004, goodwill is included on the basis of its deemed cost, which represents the amount recorded under French GAAP. The classification and accounting treatment of business combinations that occurred prior to April 1, 2004 was not modified at the time international standards were adopted, on April 1, 2004, in accordance with IFRS 1 "First-time adoption of international financial reporting standards".

Goodwill is valued in the functional currency of the entity acquired. It is recorded as an asset in the balance sheet.

It is not amortized and is tested for impairment annually and at any point during the year when an indicator of impairment exists. As discussed in Note 4.14, once recorded the impairment may not subsequently be reversed.

When the acquirer's interest in the net fair value of the identifiable assets and liabilities acquired exceeds the consideration transferred, there is negative goodwill which is recognized and immediately reversed in the Group's income statement.

At the time of the sale of a subsidiary or an equity affiliate, the amount of the goodwill attributable to the entity sold is included in the calculation of the income from the sale.

4.12 Intangible assets

Intangible assets are recorded at initial cost less accumulated amortization and any accumulated impairment losses.

Software development costs are capitalized and amortized over their useful lives. The Group has the necessary tools to enable the tracking by project of all the stages of development, and particularly the internal and external costs directly related to each project during its development phase.

Identifiable intangible assets acquired with a finite useful life are amortized over their useful lives from the date they are available for use.

Identifiable intangible assets acquired with an indefinite useful life are not amortized but tested annually for impairment or whenever there is an indication that the intangible asset may be impaired. If necessary, an impairment as described in Note 4.14 is recorded.

Since January 1, 2012, airlines have been subject to the ETS (Emission Trading Scheme) market regulations as described in Note 4.20 and the "Risks on carbon credit" paragraph in Note 34.1. As such, the Group is required to purchase CO_2 quotas to offset its emissions. The Group records the CO_2 quotas as intangible assets. These assets are not depreciable.

Intangible assets with a definite useful life are amortized on a straight line basis over the following periods:

+ software   1 to 5 years
+ customer relationships   5 to 12 years

4.13 Property, plant and equipment

4.13.1 Principles applicable

Property, plant and equipment are recorded at the acquisition or manufacturing cost, less accumulated depreciation and any accumulated impairment losses.

The financial interest attributed to progress payments made on account of aircraft and other significant assets under construction is capitalized and added to the cost of the asset concerned. As prepayments on investment are not financed by specific loans, the Group uses the average interest rate on the current unallocated loans of the period.

Maintenance costs are recorded as expenses during the period when incurred, with the exception of programs that extend the useful life of the asset or increase its value, which are then capitalized (e.g. maintenance on airframes and engines, excluding parts with limited useful lives).

4.13.2 Flight equipment

The purchase price of aircraft equipment is denominated in foreign currencies. It is translated at the exchange rate at the date of the transaction or, if applicable, at the hedging price assigned to it. Manufacturers' discounts, if any, are deducted from the value of the related asset.

Aircraft are depreciated using the straight-line method over their average estimated useful life of 20 years, assuming no residual value for most of the aircraft in the fleet. This useful life can, however, be extended to 25 years for some aircraft.

During the operating cycle, and when establishing fleet replacement plans, the Group reviews whether the amortizable base or the useful life should be adjusted and, if necessary, determines whether a residual value should be recognized.

Any major airframes and engines (excluding parts with limited useful lives) are treated as a separate asset component with the cost capitalized and depreciated over the period between the date of acquisition and the next major overhaul.

Aircraft components which enable the use of the fleet are recorded as fixed assets and are amortized on a straight-line basis over the estimated residual lifetime of the aircraft/engine type on the world market. The useful life is limited to a maximum of 30 years.

4.13.3 Other property, plant and equipment

Other property, plant and equipment are depreciated using the straight line method over their useful life. Such useful lives are as follows:

+ buildings   20 to 50 years
+ fixtures and fittings   8 to 15 years
+ flight simulators   10 to 20 years
+ equipment and tooling   5 to 15 years

4.13.4 Leases

In accordance with IAS 17 «Leases», leases are classified as finance leases when the lease arrangement transfers substantially all the risks and rewards of ownership to the lessee.

All other leases are classified as operating leases.

The assets held under a finance lease are recognized as assets at the lower of the following two values: the present value of the minimum lease payments under the lease arrangement or their fair value determined at inception of the lease. The corresponding obligation to the lessor is accounted for as long-term debt.

These assets are depreciated over the shorter of the useful life of the assets and the lease term when there is no reasonable certainty that the lessee will obtain ownership by the end of the lease term.

In the context of sale and operating leaseback transactions, the related profit or losses are accounted for as follows:

+ they are recognized immediately when it is clear that the transaction has been realized at fair value;
+ if the sale price is below fair value, any profit or loss is recognized immediately except that, if the loss is compensated for by future lease payments at below market price, it is deferred and amortized in proportion to the lease payments over the period for which the asset is expected to be used;
+ if the sale price is above fair value, the excess over fair value is deferred and amortized over the period for which the asset is expected to be used.

In the context of sale and finance leaseback transactions, the asset remains in the Group's balance sheet with the same net book value. Such transactions are a means whereby the lessor provides finance to the lessee, with the asset as security.

4.14 Impairment test

In accordance with the standard IAS 36 "Impairment of Assets", tangible fixed assets, intangible assets and goodwill are tested for depreciation if there is an indication of impairment, and those with an indefinite useful life are tested at least once a year on September 30.

For this test, the Group deems the recoverable value of the asset to be the higher of the market value less cost of disposal and its value in use. The latter is determined according to the discounted future cash flow method, estimated based on budgetary assumptions approved by management, using an actuarial rate which corresponds to the weighted average cost of the Group's capital and a growth rate which reflects the market hypotheses for the appropriate activity.

The depreciation tests are carried out individually for each asset, except for those assets to which it is not possible to attach independent cash flows. In this case, these assets are regrouped within the CGU to which they belong and it is this which is tested. The CGU relates to different activity sectors of the Group: passenger business, cargo, maintenance, leisure and others.

When the recoverable value of an asset or CGU is inferior to its net book value, an impairment is realized. The impairment of a CGU is charged in the first instance to goodwill, the remainder being charged to the other assets which comprise the CGU, prorated to their net book value.

4.15 Inventories

Inventories are measured at the lower of cost and net realizable value.

The cost of inventories comprises all costs of purchase, costs of conversion and other costs incurred in bringing the inventories to their present condition and location. These costs include the direct and indirect production costs incurred under normal operating conditions.

Inventories are valued on a weighted average basis.

The net realizable value of the inventories is the estimated selling price in the ordinary course of business less the estimated costs of completion and selling expenses.

4.16 Treasury shares

Air-France-KLM shares held by the Group are recorded as a deduction from the Group's consolidated equity at the acquisition cost. Subsequent sales are recorded directly in equity. No gains or losses are recognized in the Group's income statement.

4.17 Employee benefits

The Group's obligations in respect of defined benefit pension plans, including the termination indemnities, are calculated in accordance with IAS 19 Revised "Employee benefits", using the projected units of credit method based on actuarial assumptions and considering the specific economic conditions in each country concerned. The commitments are covered either by insurance or pension funds or by provisions recorded on the balance sheet as and when rights are acquired by employees.

The Group recognizes in Other Comprehensive Income the actuarial gains or losses relating to post-employment plans, the differential between the actual return and the expected return on the pension assets and the impact of any plan curtailment. The gains or losses relating to termination benefits are booked in the income statement.

The Group books all the costs linked to pensions (defined benefit plans and net periodic pension costs) in the income from current operations (salaries and related costs).

Specific information related to the recognition of some pension plan assets

Pension plans in the Netherlands are generally subject to minimum funding requirements ("MFR") that can involve the recognition of pension surpluses.

These pension surpluses constituted by the KLM sub group are recognized in the balance sheet according to the IFRIC 14 interpretation IAS 19 "The Limit on a Defined Benefit Asset, Minimum Funding Requirements and their Interaction".

4.18 Provisions for restitution of aircraft under operating leases

For certain operating leases, the Group is contractually committed to restitute aircraft to a defined level of potential.

The Group accrues for restitution costs related to aircraft under operating leases.

When the condition of aircraft exceeds the return condition as set per the lease arrangement, the Group capitalizes the related amount in excess under "Flight equipment". Such amounts are subsequently amortized on a straight-line basis over the period during which the potential exceeds the restitution condition. Any remaining capitalized excess potential upon termination of a lease is reimbursable by the lessor.

4.19 Other provisions

The Group recognizes a provision in the balance sheet when the Group has an existing legal or implicit obligation to a third party as a result of a past event, and it is probable that an outflow of economic benefits will be required to settle the obligation. The amounts recorded as provisions are discounted when the effect of the passage of time is material.

The effect of the time value of money is presented as a component of financial income.

Restructuring provisions are recognized once the Group has established a detailed and formal restructuring plan which has been announced to the parties concerned.

4.20 Emission Trading Scheme

Since January 2012, European airlines have been included in the scope of companies subject to the Emission Trading Scheme (ETS).

In the absence of an IFRS standard or interpretation regarding ETS accounting, the Group has adopted the accounting treatment known as the "netting approach".

According to this approach, the quotas are recognized as intangible assets:

✦ free quotas allocated by the State are valued at nil; and
✦ quotas purchased on the market are accounted at their acquisition cost.

These intangible assets are not amortized.

If the difference between recognized quotas and real emissions is negative then the Group recognizes a provision. This provision is assessed at the acquisition cost for the acquired rights and, for the non-hedged portion, with reference to the market price as of each closing date.

At the date of the restitution to the State of the quotas corresponding to real emissions, the provision is written-off in exchange for the intangible assets returned.

4.21 Equity and debt issuance costs

Debt issuance costs are mainly amortized as financial expenses over the term of the loans using the actuarial method.

The capital increase costs are deducted from paid-in capital.

4.22 Deferred taxes

The Group records deferred taxes using the balance sheet liability method, providing for any temporary differences between the carrying amounts of assets and liabilities for financial reporting purposes and the amounts used for taxation purposes, except for exceptions described in IAS 12 "Income taxes".

The tax rates used are those enacted or substantively enacted at the balance sheet date.

Net deferred tax balances are determined on the basis of each entity's tax position.

Deferred tax assets related to temporary differences and tax losses carried forward are recognized only to the extent it is probable that a future taxable profit will be available against which the asset can be utilized at the tax entity level.

Deferred tax assets corresponding to fiscal losses are recognized as assets given the prospects of recoverability resulting from budgets and medium term plans prepared by the Group. The assumptions used are similar to those used for testing the value of assets (see Note 4.14).

A deferred tax liability is also recognized for the undistributed reserves of the equity affiliates.

Taxes payable and/or deferred are recognized in the income statement for the period, unless they are generated by a transaction or event recorded directly in other comprehensive income. In such a case, they are recorded directly in other comprehensive income.

Impact of the Territorial Economic Contribution

The 2010 Finance Law voted on December 30, 2009, removed the business tax liability for French fiscal entities from January 1, 2010 and replaced it with the new TEC (Territorial Economic Contribution/ Contribution Economique Territoriale – CET) comprising two contributions: the LDE (land tax of enterprises/Cotisation Foncière des Entreprises - CFE) and the CAVE (Contribution on Added Value of Enterprises/Cotisation sur la Valeur Ajoutée des Entreprises – CVAE). The latter is calculated by the application of a rate to the added value generated by the company during the year. As the added value is a net amount of income and expenses, the CAVE meets the definition of a tax on profits as set out in IAS 12.2. Consequently, the expense relating to the CAVE is presented under the line "tax".

4.23 Non-current assets held for sale and discontinued operations

Assets or groups of assets held for sale meet the criteria of such a classification if their carrying amount is recovered principally through a sale rather than through their continuing use. This condition is considered to be met when the sale is highly probable and the asset (or the group of assets intended for sale) is available for immediate sale in its present condition. Management must be committed to a plan to sell, with the expectation that the sale will be realized within a period of twelve months from the date on which the asset or group of assets were classified as assets held for sale.

The Group determines on each closing date whether any assets or groups of assets meet the above criteria and presents such assets, if any, as "non-current assets held for sale".

Any liabilities related to these assets are also presented on a separate line in liabilities on the balance sheet.

Assets and groups of assets held for sale are valued at the lower of their book value or their fair value minus exit costs. As of the date of such a classification, the asset is no longer depreciated.

The results from discontinued operations are presented separately from the results from continuing operations in the income statement.

4.24 Share-based compensation

Stock subscription or purchase option schemes are valued at the fair value on the date the plans are awarded.

The fair value of the stock option schemes is determined using the Black-Scholes model. This model takes into account the features of the plan (exercise price, exercise period) and the market data at the time they are granted (risk-free interest rate, market value of the share, volatility and expected dividends).

This fair value is the fair value of the services rendered by the employees in consideration for the options received. It is recognized over the vesting period as salary cost with a corresponding increase to equity for transactions paid with shares and with a corresponding increase of liabilities for transactions paid in cash. During the vesting period, this salary cost is adjusted, if applicable, to take into account the number of options effectively vested.

Note 5 Change in the consolidation scope

Within the framework of the establishment of *HOP!*, the Group acquired Airlinair. This operation took place as follows:

✦ the sale, on February 28, 2013, of the shareholding in Financière LMP (39.86%), the parent company which owned Airlinair *(see Note 11)*;

✦ the acquisition, on February 28, 2013, of 100% of the Airlinair share capital for €17 million. The goodwill relating to this operation amounts to €3 million.

On May 15, 2013, the Group sold its Italian subsidiary Servair Airchef, specialized in airline catering.

As of December 31, 2013, following the Air France-KLM Group's decision not to subscribe to the capital increase requested in October 2013, the Alitalia entity is no longer consolidated by the equity method. The Group's remaining equity interest in Alitalia (7.08%) is recorded under other financial assets *(see Notes 3, 11, 22 and 24)*.

Note 6 Segment information

Business segments

The segment information by activity and geographical area presented below is prepared on the basis of internal management data communicated to the Executive Committee, the Group's principal operational decision-making body.

The Group is organized around the following segments:

✦ **Passenger**: Passenger operating revenues primarily come from passenger transportation services on scheduled flights with the

Group's airline code, including flights operated by other airlines under code-sharing agreements. They also include commissions paid by SkyTeam alliance partners, code-sharing revenues, revenues from excess baggage, airport services supplied by the Group to third-party airlines and services linked to IT systems;

✦ **Cargo**: Cargo operating revenues come from freight transport on flights under the companies' codes, including flights operated by other partner airlines under code-sharing agreements. Other cargo revenues are derived principally from sales of cargo capacity to third parties.

✦ **Maintenance**: Maintenance operating revenues are generated through maintenance services provided to other airlines and customers globally;

✦ **Other**: The revenues from this segment come primarily from catering supplied by the Group to third-party airlines and from charter flights operated primarily by Transavia.

The results, assets and liabilities allocated to the business segments correspond to those attributable directly and indirectly. Amounts allocated to business segments mainly correspond, for the income statement, to the income from operating activities and for the balance sheet, to the goodwill, intangible assets, flight equipment and other tangible assets, the share in equity affiliates, some account receivables, deferred revenue on ticket sales and a portion of provisions and retirement benefits. Other elements of the income statement and balance sheet are presented in the "non-allocated" column.

Inter-segment transactions are evaluated based on normal market conditions.

Geographical segments

The Group's activities are broken down into six geographical regions:

✦ Metropolitan France;
✦ Europe (excluding France) and North Africa;
✦ Caribbean, French Guiana and Indian Ocean;
✦ Africa, Middle East;
✦ Americas, Polynesia;
✦ Asia and New Caledonia.

Only segment revenue is allocated by geographical sales area.

The carrying amount of segment assets by geographical location and the costs incurred to acquire segment assets are not presented, since most of the Group's assets (flight equipment) cannot be allocated to a geographical area.

6.1 Information by business segment

➤ **Year ended December 31, 2013**

(In € million)	Passenger	Cargo	Maintenance	Other	Non-allocated	Total
Total sales	21,578	2,849	3,280	1,980	-	29,687
Inter-segment sales	(1,466)	(33)	(2,055)	(613)	-	(4,167)
External sales	*20,112*	*2,816*	*1,225*	*1,367*	*-*	*25,520*
Income from current operations	174	(202)	159	(1)	-	130
Income from operating activities	(39)	(343)	146	9	-	(227)
Share of profits (losses) of associates	(215)	-	2	2	-	(211)
Net cost of financial debt and other financial income and expenses	-	-	-	-	(301)	(301)
Income taxes	-	-	-	-	(957)	(957)
Net income from continuing operations	*(254)*	*(343)*	*148*	*11*	*(1,258)*	*(1,696)*
Depreciation and amortization for the period	(1,062)	(71)	(277)	(156)	-	(1,566)
Other non monetary items	(385)	(78)	(43)	(200)	(835)	(1,541)
Total assets	**11,089**	**1,052**	**2,671**	**862**	**9,749**	**25,423**
Segment liabilities	6,341	281	713	367	4,532	12,234
Financial debt, bank overdraft and equity	-	-	-	-	13,189	13,189
Total liabilities	**6,341**	**281**	**713**	**367**	**17,721**	**25,423**
Purchase of property, plant and equipment and intangible assets (continuing operations)	*829*	*44*	*188*	*125*	*-*	*1,186*

Non-allocated assets, amounting to €9.7 billion, are mainly financial assets held by the Group. They especially comprise cash and cash equivalent for €3.7 billion, pension assets for €2.5 billion, financial assets for €2.7 billion, deferred tax for €0.4 billion and derivatives for €0.4 billion.

Non-allocated liabilities, amounting to €4.5 billion, mainly comprise a portion of provisions and retirement benefits for €2.3 billion, tax and employee-related liabilities for €1.2 billion, deferred tax for €0.2 billion and derivatives for €0.4 billion.

Financial debts, bank overdrafts and equity are not allocated.

➤ **Year ended December 31, 2012 (pro forma)**

(In € million)	Passenger	Cargo	Maintenance	Other	Non-allocated	Total
Total sales	21,495	3,084	3,134	1,901	-	29,614
Inter-segment sales	(1,519)	(27)	(2,038)	(607)	-	(4,191)
External sales	*19,976*	*3,057*	*1,096*	*1,294*	*-*	*25,423*
Income from current operations	(260)	(230)	140	14	-	(336)
Income from operating activities	(518)	(333)	104	16	-	(731)
Share of profits (losses) of associates	(72)	1	1	4	-	(66)
Net cost of financial debt and other financial income and expenses	-	-	-	-	(209)	(209)
Income taxes	-	-	-	-	(17)	(17)
Net income from continuing operations	*(590)*	*(332)*	*105*	*20*	*(226)*	*(1,023)*
Depreciation and amortization for the period	(1,079)	(69)	(278)	(150)	-	(1,576)
Other non monetary items	(1,521)	(106)	(61)	5	160	(1,523)
Total assets	**11,386**	**1,177**	**2,679**	**1,499**	**9,979**	**26,720**
Segment liabilities	6,034	276	713	835	3,969	11,827
Financial debt, bank overdraft and equity	-	-	-	-	14,893	14,893
Total liabilities	**6,034**	**276**	**713**	**835**	**18,862**	**26,720**
Purchase of property, plant and equipment and intangible assets (continuing operations)	*1,105*	*36*	*201*	*123*	*-*	*1,465*

Non-allocated assets, amounting to €10 billion, were mainly financial assets held by the Group. They comprise marketable securities for €3.8 billion, pension assets for €2.5 billion, financial assets for €1.4 billion, deferred tax for €1.4 billion, cash for €0.6 billion and derivatives for €0.3 billion.

Non-allocated liabilities, amounting to €4 billion, mainly comprised a portion of provisions and retirement benefits for €2.4 billion, tax and employee-related liabilities for €1.1 billion, deferred tax for €0.1 billion and derivatives for €0.4 billion.

Financial debts, bank overdrafts and equity are not allocated.

6.2 Information by geographical area

Sales by geographical area

➤ Year ended December 31, 2013

(In € million)	Metropolitan France	Europe (except France) North Africa	Caribbean, French Guiana, Indian Ocean	Africa, Middle East	Americas, Polynesia	Asia, New Caledonia	Total
Scheduled passenger	5,818	6,002	364	1,286	3,596	2,110	19,176
Other passenger sales	399	302	15	56	64	100	936
Total passenger	6,217	6,304	379	1,342	3,660	2,210	20,112
Scheduled cargo	388	1,026	26	177	443	559	2,619
Other cargo sales	55	33	4	17	47	41	197
Total cargo	443	1,059	30	194	490	600	2,816
Maintenance	749	442	-	-	34	-	1,225
Other	466	803	33	65	-	-	1,367
Total	7,875	8,608	442	1,601	4,184	2,810	25,520

➤ Year ended December 31, 2012 (pro forma)

(In € million)	Metropolitan France	Europe (except France) North Africa	Caribbean, French Guiana, Indian Ocean	Africa, Middle East	Americas, Polynesia	Asia, New Caledonia	Total
Scheduled passenger	5,799	6,171	365	1,263	3,403	2,064	19,065
Other passenger sales	359	303	14	61	60	114	911
Total passenger	6,158	6,474	379	1,324	3,463	2,178	19,976
Scheduled cargo	372	1,123	30	206	524	617	2,872
Other cargo sales	51	49	4	10	41	30	185
Total cargo	423	1,172	34	216	565	647	3,057
Maintenance	709	351	-	-	36	-	1,096
Other	400	805	29	59	-	1	1,294
Total	7,690	8,802	442	1,599	4,064	2,826	25,423

Traffic sales by geographical area of destination

➤ **Year ended December 31, 2013**

(In € million)	Metropolitan France	Europe (except France) North Africa	Caribbean, French Guiana, Indian Ocean	Africa, Middle East	Americas, Polynesia	Asia, New Caledonia	Total
Scheduled passenger	1,932	4,466	1,421	2,538	5,397	3,422	19,176
Scheduled cargo	5	46	142	524	1,053	849	2,619
Total	**1,937**	**4,512**	**1,563**	**3,062**	**6,450**	**4,271**	**21,795**

➤ **Year ended December 31, 2012 (pro forma)**

(In € million)	Metropolitan France	Europe (except France) North Africa	Caribbean, French Guiana, Indian Ocean	Africa, Middle East	Americas, Polynesia	Asia, New Caledonia	Total
Scheduled passenger	1,970	4,438	1,401	2,567	5,248	3,441	19,065
Scheduled cargo	5	49	148	603	1,168	899	2,872
Total	**1,975**	**4,487**	**1,549**	**3,170**	**6,416**	**4,340**	**21,937**

Note 7 External expenses

Period from 1 January to 31 December (In € million)	2013	2012 Pro forma
Aircraft fuel	6,897	7,278
Chartering costs	455	551
Aircraft operating lease costs	913	949
Landing fees and en route charges	1,839	1,832
Catering	589	591
Handling charges and other operating costs	1,405	1,368
Aircraft maintenance costs	1,303	1,131
Commercial and distribution costs	852	866
Other external expenses	1,744	1,706
Total	**15,997**	**16,272**
Excluding aircraft fuel	*9,100*	*8,994*

Note 8 Salaries and number of employees

Salaries and related costs

Period from January 1 to December 31 *(In € million)*	2013	2012 Pro forma
Wages and salaries	5,424	5,514
Costs linked to defined contribution plans	603	610
Net periodic pension cost	379	359
Social contributions	1,171	1,207
Expenses related to share-based compensation	3	5
Other expenses	(98)	(33)
Total	**7,482**	**7,662**

The Group pays contributions to a multi-employer plan in France, the CRPN (public pension fund for crew). This multi-employer plan being assimilated with a French State plan, it is accounted for as a defined contribution plan in "social contributions".

The "other expenses" notably comprise:

+ the CICE tax credit amounting to €43 million as of December 31, 2013;
+ the capitalization of salary costs on aircraft and engine overhaul.

Average number of employees on continuing operations

Year ended December 31	2013	2012 Pro forma
Flight deck crew	8,103	8,157
Cabin crew	21,779	22,104
Ground staff	66,535	69,639
Total	**96,417**	**99,900**

Note 9   Amortization, depreciation and provisions

Period from January 1 to December 31 *(In € million)*	2013	2012 Pro forma
Intangible assets	80	67
Flight equipment	1,227	1,238
Other property, plant and equipment	259	271
Amortization	*1,566*	*1,576*
Inventories	(1)	-
Trade receivables	5	(1)
Risks and contingencies	155	155
Depreciation and provisions	*159*	*154*
Total	**1,725**	**1,730**

The impact of the review of the useful lives of some aircraft on the value of amortization amounted to €(29) million as of December 31, 2012.

The amortization changes for intangible and tangible assets are presented in Notes 18 and 20.

The changes in impairment relating to inventories and trade receivables are presented in Notes 25, 26 and 27.

The movements in provisions for risks and charges are detailed in Note 31.

Note 10   Other income and expenses

Period from January 1 to December 31 *(In € million)*	2013	2012 Pro forma
Joint operation of routes	(84)	(39)
Operations-related currency hedges	65	117
Other	9	(5)
Total	**(10)**	**73**

Note 11 Other non-current income and expenses

Period from January 1 to December 31 *(In € million)*	2013	2012 Pro forma
Sales of aircraft equipment	*(12)*	*8*
Restructuring costs	(209)	(455)
Depreciation of assets available for sale	(102)	-
Disposals of subsidiaries and affiliates	7	97
Impairment on goodwill	-	(5)
Other	(41)	(40)
Total	*(345)*	*(403)*

Period from January 1 to December 31, 2013

▌ *Restructuring costs*

During the third quarter 2013, the Group announced the implementation of additional measures to reduce Air France's salary costs. The overstaffing was estimated at 2,880 employees, including 1,826 for ground staff. In this context, a voluntary departure plan is proposed to ground staff and cabin crew, whose application period will open in 2014.

During the financial year, the Group also adjusted the amount of the net provision booked as of December 31, 2012 concerning the initial voluntary departure plan and the resizing of the fleet.

The Group has consequently made its best estimate of the costs incurred by the measures mentioned above and has recorded a restructuring provision for a total amount of €200 million as of December 31, 2013.

A provision for an onerous lease contract on a Martinair Boeing B747 has also been recorded for an amount of €9 million.

▌ *Depreciation of assets available for sale*

As part of the review of its fleet plan, the Air France Group has decided to sell two Boeing B747s freighters. The impact of the revaluation of these non-operated aircraft on their sale amounts to €82 million *(see Note 15)*.

For its part, the KLM Group has revalued seven Fokker F70s, two MD11s, one Fokker F100 and several engines at their sale value, representing a total amount of €20 million.

▌ *Disposal of subsidiaries and affiliates*

This line includes:

✦ the sale of the shareholding in Financière LMP (39.86%) *(see Note 5);*
✦ the sale of the shareholding in Servair Airchef (50%) *(see Note 5);*
✦ the impact of dilution on the Alitalia shareholding *(see Notes 3, 5, 22 and 24).*

▌ *Other*

This line mainly includes:

✦ a provision of €18 million relating to crew disputes;
✦ an additional provision related to anti-competitive cargo practices amounting to €14 million *(see Note 31.3);*
✦ an exceptional tax on salaries in the Netherlands, linked to the economic crisis in Europe, amounting to €7 million.

Period from January 1 to December 31, 2012

▌ *Restructuring costs*

The Group initiated a restructuring plan concerning all the Group companies, comprising mostly two parts: a fleet capacity adjustment and a plan to reduce staff.

Concerning the Air France Group, the plan's conditions were presented to the employee representative bodies of Air France in June 2012 and to its affiliates during the fourth quarter of 2012.

Concerning the resizing of the fleet, the modalities may result, for the equipment involved, in the disposal, sale or dismantling of aircraft or the termination of operating lease contracts.

The Air France staff reduction plan concerning 5,122 positions included assistance for voluntary retirement and a voluntary departure plan whose period of application had opened during the fourth quarter of 2012.

Concerning KLM, a resizing of the fleet was carried out, resulting in the booking of fair value for the MD11 aircraft which were withdrawn from operation.

Given the items mentioned above, the Group had made its best estimate of the costs incurred by these measures and had recorded a provision for restructuring amounting to €408 million as of December 31, 2012.

This provision has been updated as the conditions modalities evolved.

A provision for onerous lease contracts on three Martinair Boeing B747s had also been recorded amounting to €50 million.

❚ *Disposals of subsidiaries and affiliates*

The "disposals of subsidiaries and affiliates" line included €97 million corresponding to the gain on disposal realised by the Group on March 1, 2012 concerning a private placement of Amadeus IT Holding SA shares, whose sale proceeds amounted to €466 million.

❚ *Other*

The "other" line mainly included:

✦ an exceptional tax on salaries in the Netherlands, linked to the economic crisis in Europe, amounting to €17 million;

✦ an additional provision related to anti-competitive cargo practices in Switzerland, Brazil and the United States amounting to €20 million *(see Note 31.3)*.

Note 12 Net cost of financial debt and other financial income and expenses

Period from January 1 to December 31 *(In € million)*	2013	2012
Income from marketable securities	26	28
Other financial income	51	55
Financial income	*77*	*83*
Loan interests	(290)	(269)
Lease interests	(75)	(87)
Capitalized interests	9	14
Other financial expenses	(125)	(94)
Cost of financial debt	*(481)*	*(436)*
Net cost of financial debt	*(404)*	*(353)*
Foreign exchange gains (losses), net	74	64
Change in fair value of financial assets and liabilities	57	63
✦ *Including fuel derivatives*	*84*	*61*
✦ *Including currency derivatives*	*(30)*	*(27)*
✦ *Including interest rates derivatives*	*4*	*(10)*
✦ *Including other derivatives*	*(1)*	*39*
Net charge release to provisions	(30)	15
Other	2	2
Other financial income and expenses	*103*	*144*
Total	**(301)**	**(209)**

The interest rate used in the calculation of capitalized interest is 3.8% for the year ended December 31, 2013 versus 4% for the year ended December 31, 2012.

Financial income mainly comprises interest income and gains on the sale of financial assets at fair value through profit and loss.

As of December 31, 2013, the cost of financial debt includes an amount of €41 million corresponding to the difference between the nominal interest rate and the effective interest rate (after split

accounting of the OCEANEs bonds issued), against €24 million as of December 31, 2012.

As of December 31, 2012, the Group had recorded under change in fair value of financial assets and liabilities (line "Other derivatives") a financial income amounting to €38 million linked to the swap on the OCEANE 2005 *(see Note 32.2.1)*.

Note 13 Income taxes

13.1 Income tax expense

Current income tax expenses and deferred income tax are detailed as follows:

Period from January 1 to December 31 *(In € million)*	2013	2012 Pro forma
(Expense) / income for the year	(41)	(41)
Current tax (expense) / income	*(41)*	*(41)*
Change in temporary differences	20	(50)
CAVE impact	3	3
Tax loss carryforwards	(939)	71
Deferred tax income / (expense) from continuing operations	*(916)*	*24*
Total	**(957)**	**(17)**

The current tax expense relates to the amounts paid or payable in the short term to the tax authorities in respect of the financial year, in accordance with the regulations prevailing in the different countries and any applicable treaties.

In France, tax losses can be carried forward for an unlimited period. However, the 2011 and 2012 Finance Acts limited the amount of the fiscal loss recoverable each year to 50% of the profit for the period beyond the first million. The period for recovering these losses against future profits having also been extended within the context of prevailing economic crisis and a highly competitive global market, the Group decided, for reasons of prudence, to limit on an appropriate period its

recoverability horizon relating to the French fiscal group. The amount of deferred tax assets relating to tax losses has consequently been reduced to €708 million as of December 31, 2013, against €1,645 million as of December 31, 2012.

In the Netherlands, tax losses can be carried forward for a period of nine years, without any limit on the amount that can be recovered in any one year.

During the year ended December 31, 2012, the Group had recognized deferred tax assets on fiscal losses of €71 million, mainly relating to the Dutch fiscal group.

13.2 Deferred tax recorded directly in equity – Group

Period from January 1 to December 31 *(In € million)*	2013	2012 Pro forma
Treasury shares	-	(3)
OCEANE	(37)	-
Other comprehensive income that will be reclassified to profit or loss	(10)	30
♦ *Assets available for sale*	*(18)*	*(4)*
♦ *Derivatives*	*8*	*34*
Other comprehensive income that will not be reclassified to profit or loss	(18)	95
♦ *Pensions*	*(18)*	*95*
Total	**(65)**	**122**

13.3 Effective tax rate

The difference between the standard tax rate in France and the effective tax rate is detailed as follows:

Period from January 1 to December 31 (In € million)	2013	2012 Pro forma
Income before tax	(528)	(940)
Standard tax rate in France	34.43%	34.43%
Theoretical tax calculated with the standard tax rate in France	182	324
Differences in French / foreign tax rates	16	(2)
Non deductible expenses or non taxable income	(20)	2
Variation of unrecognized deferred tax assets	(1,135)	(317)
CAVE impact	(24)	(21)
Other	24	(3)
Income tax expenses	**(957)**	**(17)**
Effective tax rate	NS	NS

The current tax rate applicable in France is 38% within 2014 including additional contributions. Since the French fiscal group realized a fiscal deficit as of December 31, 2013, the taxproof has been established using the rate excluding additional contributions, i.e. 34.43%. Deferred tax has been calculated on the same basis.

The current tax rate applicable in the Netherlands is 25%.

13.4 Deferred tax recorded on the balance sheet

(In € million)	January 1, 2013	Amounts recorded in income	Amounts recorded in OCI	Amounts recorded in equity	Currency translation adjustment	Reclassification and other	December 31, 2013
Flight equipment	(1,257)	(15)	-	-	-	(5)	(1,277)
Pension assets	(566)	(47)	14	-	-	(9)	(608)
Financial debt	758	60	-	(37)	-	(1)	780
Deferred revenue on ticket sales	166	11	-	-	-	-	177
Others	(14)	14	(42)	-	-	(1)	(43)
Deferred tax corresponding to fiscal losses	2,156	(939)	-	-	-	12	1,229
Deferred tax asset / (liability)	**1,243**	**(916)**	**(28)**	**(37)**	**-**	**(4)**	**258**

Deferred taxes recognized on fiscal losses for the French and Dutch fiscal perimeters amount to €1,178 million as of December 31, 2013 (€708 million for the French fiscal group and €470 million for the Dutch fiscal group).

The recognition of this asset for each of the two perimeters is based on the prospects for taxable income established by the Group's three-year plan and based on the same assumptions as those outlined in Note 19 "Impairment" to these consolidated financial statements.

Based on these prospects for taxable income, the recoverability horizon is suitable as for the French perimeter than for the Dutch perimeter. The non realization of these assumptions could have a significant impact on the recoverability horizon for these deferred tax assets.

(In € million)	January 1, 2012 Pro forma	Amounts recorded in income	Amounts recorded in OCI	Amounts recorded in equity	Currency translation adjustment	Reclassification and other	December 31, 2012 Pro forma
Flight equipment	(1,147)	(110)	-	-	-	-	(1,257)
Pension assets	(530)	(43)	7	-	-	-	(566)
Financial debt	614	144	-	-	-	-	758
Other liabilities	84	(55)	44	-	-	-	73
Deferred revenue on ticket sales	170	(4)	-	-	-	-	166
Others	(176)	18	74	(3)	-	-	(87)
Deferred tax corresponding to fiscal losses	2,085	71	-	-	-	-	2,156
Deferred tax asset / (liability)	**1,100**	**21**	**125**	**(3)**	**-**	**-**	**1,243**

Deferred tax recognized on fiscal losses for the French and Dutch fiscal perimeters amounted to €2,100 million as of December 31, 2012 (€1,645 million for the French fiscal group and €455 million for the Dutch fiscal group).

13.5 Unrecognized deferred tax assets

(In € million)	December 31, 2013		December 31, 2012	
	Basis	Tax	Basis	Tax
Temporary differences	476	164	469	159
Tax losses	4,025	1,386	755	260
Total	**4,501**	**1,550**	**1,224**	**419**

As of December 31, 2013, the cumulative effect of the limitation the French fiscal group's deferred tax assets results in the non-recognition of a deferred tax asset amounting to €1,525 million (corresponding to a basis of €4,429 million), including €1,362 million relating to tax losses and €163 million relating to temporary differences (non-recognition of deferred tax assets relating to restructuration provisions). The amount of deferred tax on tax losses non recognized during the period includes €937 million relating to the limitation of the recoverability horizon (see Note 13.1).

As of December 31, 2012, the cumulative effect of the limitation the French fiscal group's deferred tax assets resulted in the non-recognition of a deferred tax asset amounting to €394 million (corresponding to a basis of €1,144 million), including €239 million relating to tax losses and €155 million relating to temporary differences (non-recognition of deferred tax assets relating to restructuration provisions).

Other unrecognized deferred tax assets mainly correspond to a portion of the tax loss carry-forwards of the Air France Group subsidiaries, as well as tax loss carryforwards in some subsidiairies in the United Kingdom.

Note 14 Net income from discontinued operations

The line "Net income from discontinued operations" corresponds to the contribution of the all CityJet and VLM

Period from January 1 to December 31 *(In millions of euros)*	2013	2012 Pro forma
Sales	*150*	*210*
Income from current operations	*(19)*	*(17)*
Impairment	(77)	(168)
Other non current items	(25)	(4)
Income from operating activities	*(121)*	*(189)*
Financial income	(1)	(5)
Income before taxes	(122)	(194)
Income taxes	-	(3)
Net income from discontinued operations	**(122)**	**(197)**

Period from January 1 to December 31, 2013

❚ *Impairment*

Within the framework of the valuation of the Irish and Belgian "regional" companies, the Group recorded an additional provision of €77 million, to align the net assets of the CityJet and VLM Group with its expected sale value.

❚ *Other non current items*

The other non current items include provisions regarding a breach of contract and disputes relating to the payment of social contributions in France.

Period from January 1 to December 31, 2012

❚ *Impairment*

Within the framework of the "Transform 2015" restructuring plan as presented at the end of August 2012 to the Works Councils of the relevant companies, the Air France Group decided to reorganize its "regional" activity by regrouping the French subsidiaries in Hop! and separating them from the other regional airlines, particularly in Ireland and Belgium.

Within this framework, the Group reviewed the assets of CityJet and its subsidiary VLM, which are now valued on a stand-alone basis. In 2012, this review prompted the Group to depreciate all the goodwill attached to VLM, amounting to €168 million.

Note 15 Assets held for sale and liabilities related to assets held for sale

Year ended December 31, 2013

As of December 31, 2013, the "Assets held for sale" and "Liabilities related to assets held for sale" correspond, for a respective €34 million and €58 million, to the assets and liabilities of the CityJet Group held for sale *(see Notes 2 and 14)*.

Furthermore, the line "Assets held for sale" includes the fair value of six aircraft held for sale for an amount of €57 million, including two Boeing B747 freighters in the Air France Group for €51 million *(see Note 11)*.

Year ended December 31, 2012

As of December 31, 2012, the line "assets held for sale" included the fair value of six aircraft held for sale for an amount of €7 million.

Note 16 Earnings per share

16.1 Income for the period – Equity holders of Air France-KLM per share

Reconciliation of income used to calculate earnings per share

The result used to calculate earnings per share are as follows:

As of January 1 to December 31 *(In € million)*	2013	2012 Pro forma
Net income- Equity holders of Air France-KLM	(1,827)	(1,225)
Net income from continuing operations - Equity holders of Air France-KLM	(1,705)	(1,028)
Net income from discontinued operations - Equity holders of Air France-KLM	(122)	(197)

Since the Group does not pay dividends to preferred stockholders, there is no difference with the results appearing in the financial statements. The results being losses for the periods presented, the results used to calculate diluted earnings per share are to the same as the results used to calculate earnings per share.

Reconciliation of the number of shares used to calculate earnings per share

Year ended to December 31	2013	2012
Weighted average number of:		
◆ Ordinary shares issued	300,219,278	300,219,278
◆ Treasury stock held regarding stock option plan	(1,116,420)	(1,116,420)
◆ Treasury stock held in stock buyback plan	-	(159,712)
◆ Other treasury stock	(3,067,607)	(3,073,029)
Number of shares used to calculate basic earnings per share	*296,035,251*	*295,870,117*
OCEANE conversion	-	-
Number of ordinary and potential ordinary shares used to calculate diluted earnings per share	*296,035,251*	*295,870,117*

16.2 Non dilutive instruments

The Air France-KLM Group did not own any non dilutive instrument as of December 31, 2013.

16.3 Instruments issued after the closing date

No instruments were issued after the closing date.

Note 17 Goodwill

Detail of consolidated goodwill

As of December 31 (In € million)	2013			2012		
	Gross value	Impairment	Net value	Gross value	Impairment	Net value
VLM	-	-	-	168	(168)	-
UTA	112	-	112	112	-	112
Régional	60	-	60	60	-	60
Aeromaintenance Group	20	(3)	17	21	(4)	17
Britair	20	-	20	20	-	20
CityJet	-	-	-	11	-	11
NAS Airport Services Limited	22	-	22	24	(1)	23
Other	7	(1)	6	10	(1)	9
Total	**241**	**(4)**	**237**	**426**	**(174)**	**252**

The goodwill concerns mainly the "Passenger" business.

Movement in net book value of goodwill

As of December 31 (In € million)	2013	2012
Opening balance	**252**	**426**
Acquisitions	3	-
Disposals	(6)	-
Impairment	(11)	(173)
Currency translation adjustment	(1)	(1)
Closing balance	**237**	**252**

As of December 31, 2013, the impairment recorded concerns CityJet, following the writing down of its net asset value on its reclassification under assets available for sale *(see Note 2.2)*.

As of December 31, 2012, the impairment recorded mainly concerned the VLM goodwill. Within the framework of the «Transform 2015» restructuring plan, the Group proceeded to review the assets of CityJet and its subsidiary VLM as described in Note 14. This review had led the Group to depreciate all the goodwill attached to VLM amounting to €168 million. The related expense was recognized in non-current expenses in the income statement.

Note 18 Intangible assets

(In € million)	Trademarks and slots	Customer relationships	Other intangible assets	Total
Gross value				
Amount as of December 31, 2011	*297*	*107*	*825*	*1,229*
Additions	-	-	146	**146**
Change in scope	-	-	-	**-**
Disposals	-	-	(25)	**(25)**
Transfer	-	-	(4)	**(4)**
Amount as of December 31, 2012	*297*	*107*	*942*	*1,346*
Additions	-	-	166	**166**
Change in scope	-	-	(6)	**(6)**
Disposals	-	-	(32)	**(32)**
Transfer	(4)	-	(4)	**(8)**
Amount as of December 31, 2013	*293*	*107*	*1,066*	*1,466*
Depreciation				
Amount as of December 31, 2011	*(2)*	*(102)*	*(351)*	*(455)*
Charge to depreciation	-	-	(68)	**(68)**
Releases on disposal	-	-	19	**19**
Transfer	-	-	-	**-**
Amount as of December 31, 2012	*(2)*	*(102)*	*(400)*	*(504)*
Charge to depreciation	(1)	(2)	(73)	**(76)**
Releases on disposal	-	-	5	**5**
Change in scope	-	-	5	**5**
Amount as of December 31, 2013	*(3)*	*(104)*	*(463)*	*(570)*
Net value				
As of December 31, 2012	295	5	542	**842**
As of December 31, 2013	290	3	603	**896**

Intangible assets mainly comprise:

+ the KLM and Transavia brands and slots (takeoff and landing) acquired by the Group as part of the acquisition of KLM. These intangible assets have an indefinite useful life as the nature of the assets means they have no time limit;

+ software and capitalized IT costs.

Note 19 Impairment

Concerning the methodology followed to test impairment, the Group has allocated each item of goodwill and each intangible fixed asset with an indefinite useful life to Cash Generating Units (CGU), corresponding to their business segments (see "Accounting Policies").

As of December 31, 2013, goodwill and intangible fixed assets with an indefinite useful life were attached principally to the "Passenger" CGU for €194 million and €288 million respectively.

The recoverable value of the CGU assets has been determined by reference to their value in use as of September 30, 2013, except for the Cargo CGU for which an additional test has been made as of December 31, 2013. The tests were realized for all the CGUs on the basis of a three-year Group plan, approved by the management, including a recovery hypothesis after the economic slowdown, enabling the achievement of the medium-term forecasts made by the Group before the emergence of the crisis.

The discount rate used for the test corresponds to the Group's weighted average cost of capital (WACC). It amounts to 7.4% at December 31, 2013 against 7.7% at December 31, 2012.

After this test, no impairment was observed on the Group's CGUs.

The Cargo CGU being loss-making, the Group has also tested all the tangible assets of this business as of December 31, 2013. No impairment was observed.

The asset value of Cargo CGU, which amounts to €715 millions, is covered by its future free cash flows. A decrease of 50 basis points in the percentage of the current operations margin target would lead to record an impairment loss of approximately €100 million. An increase of 50 basis points of the discount rate would lead to record an impairment loss of approximately €60 million.

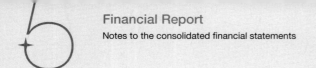

Note 20 Tangible assets

(In € million)	Flight equipment					Other tangible assets					Total
	Owned aircraft	Leased aircraft	Assets in progress	Other	Total	Land and buildings	Equipment and machinery	Assets in progress	Other	Total	
Gross value											
As of December 31, 2011	*10,872*	*5,216*	*728*	*2,143*	*18,959*	*2,673*	*1,288*	*100*	*908*	*4,969*	*23,928*
Acquisitions	351	161	764	105	1,381	46	51	55	29	181	**1,562**
Disposals	(922)	(77)	(63)	(150)	(1,212)	(41)	(23)	-	(27)	(91)	**(1,303)**
Fair value	-	-	48	-	48	-	-	-	-	-	**48**
Transfer	(480)	883	(1,130)	37	(690)	64	10	(100)	15	(11)	**(701)**
As of December 31, 2012	*9,821*	*6,183*	*347*	*2,135*	*18,486*	*2,742*	*1,326*	*55*	*925*	*5,048*	*23,534*
Acquisitions	133	4	705	109	951	48	22	70	20	160	**1,111**
Disposals	(732)	(79)	-	(188)	(999)	(16)	(16)	-	(15)	(47)	**(1,046)**
Scope variation	20	36	-	-	56	-	-	-	(6)	(6)	**50**
Fair value	-	-	54	-	54	-	-	-	-	-	**54**
Transfer	(380)	588	(706)	107	(391)	54	-	(30)	(41)	(17)	**(408)**
Currency translation adjustment	-	-	-	-	-	-	(1)	-	(1)	(2)	**(2)**
As of December 31, 2013	*8,862*	*6,732*	*400*	*2,163*	*18,157*	*2,828*	*1,331*	*95*	*882*	*5,136*	*23,293*
Depreciation											
As of December 31, 2011	*(5,695)*	*(1,645)*	*-*	*(930)*	*(8,270)*	*(1,422)*	*(834)*	*-*	*(658)*	*(2,914)*	*(11,184)*
Charge to depreciation	(800)	(364)	-	(128)	(1,292)	(134)	(82)	-	(56)	(272)	**(1,564)**
Releases on disposal	286	73	-	134	493	34	20	-	15	69	**562**
Transfer	721	(111)	-	21	631	(1)	-	-	2	1	**632**
As of December 31, 2012	*(5,488)*	*(2,047)*	*-*	*(903)*	*(8,438)*	*(1,523)*	*(896)*	*-*	*(697)*	*(3,116)*	*(11,554)*
Charge to depreciation	(788)	(405)	-	(144)	(1,337)	(132)	(80)	-	(48)	(260)	**(1,597)**
Releases on disposal	518	76	-	162	756	15	13	-	8	36	**792**
Scope variation	-	-	-	-	-	-	-	-	3	3	**3**
Transfer	423	(113)	-	(57)	253	(28)	13	-	34	19	**272**
Currency translation adjustment	-	-	-	-	-	-	1	-	-	1	**1**
As of December 31, 2013	*(5,335)*	*(2,489)*	*-*	*(942)*	*(8,766)*	*(1,668)*	*(949)*	*-*	*(700)*	*(3,317)*	*(12,083)*
Net value											
As of December 31, 2012	4,333	4,136	347	1,232	**10,048**	1,219	430	55	228	**1,932**	11,980
As of December 31, 2013	3,527	4,243	400	1,221	**9,391**	1,160	382	95	182	**1,819**	11,210

Aeronautical assets under construction mainly include advance payments, maintenance work in progress concerning engines and aircraft modifications.

Note 37 details the amount of pledged tangible assets.

Commitments to property purchases are detailed in Notes 37 and 38.

The net book value of tangible assets financed under capital lease amounts to €4,762 million as of December 31, 2013 versus €4,618 million as of December 31, 2012.

The charge to depreciation as of December 31, 2013 includes €102 million of depreciation booked in non current charges *(see Note 11)*.

The charge to depreciation as of December 31, 2012 included €40 million relating to the resizing of the Group's fleet, booked in restructuring costs *(see Note 11)*.

Note 21 Capital expenditure

The detail of capital expenditures on tangible and intangible assets presented in the consolidated cash flow statements is as follows:

As of December 31 *(In € million)*	2013	2012
Acquisition of tangible assets	1,046	1,351
Acquisition of intangible assets	166	146
Accounts payable on acquisitions and capitalized interest	(26)	(32)
Total	**1,186**	**1,465**

Note 22 Equity affiliates

Movements over the period

The table below presents the movement in equity affiliates:

(In € million)	Alitalia	Kenya Airways	Other	Total
Carrying value of share in investment as of December 31, 2011	**274**	**57**	**91**	**422**
Share in net income of equity affiliates	(61)	(12)	7	(66)
Distributions	-	(1)	(3)	(4)
Change in consolidation scope	-	1	2	3
Fair value adjustment	(6)	(2)	-	(8)
Other variations	-	36	1	37
Currency translation adjustment	-	(3)	-	(3)
Carrying value of share in investment as of December 31, 2012 (pro forma)	**207**	**76**	**98**	**381**
Share in net income of equity affiliates	(202)	(8)	(1)	(211)
Distributions	-	-	(2)	(2)
Change in consolidation scope	-	-	(11)	(11)
Other variations	-	4	7	11
Fair value adjustment	(5)	-	-	(5)
Capital increase	-	-	16	16
Currency translation adjustment	-	(2)	-	(2)
Carrying value of share in investment as of December 31, 2013	**-**	**70**	**107**	**177**
Market value for listed companies		45		

Following the dilution in its shareholding during the last quarter of 2013, the Group no longer accounts for Alitalia as an equity affiliate, but now recognizes its equity interest under other financial assets *(see Notes 3, 5, 11 and 24)*.

Given the uncertainties overhanging Alitalia's situation prior to this dilution in its shareholding, the Group decided, during the third quarter, to totally depreciate its shareholding in Alitalia. The share of losses and a provision for impairment have consequently been booked amounting to a total of €202 million.

Simplified financial statements of the main equity affiliates

The investments in equity affiliates as of December 31, 2013 mainly concern the company Kenya Airways, a Kenyan airline based in Nairobi, over which the Group exercises a significant influence.

As of December 31, 2012, besides Kenya Airways, investments in equity affiliates also included the company Alitalia Aerea Italiana Spa. This entity, which began operations on January 12, 2009, is derived from the contribution of the transition from the old Alitalia and redemption of Air One activity. It was removed from the equity affiliates scope during the last quarter of 2013 following the Group's decision not to subscribe to the requested capital increase. Since this date, Alitalia's shares are recognized in other financial assets.

The financial statements of the main equity affiliates are presented below.

They correspond to 100% of the financial data for the years 2013 and 2012, prepared in accordance with the local standards of the relevant host countries.

(In € million)	Alitalia 12/31/2012	Kenya Airways 03/31/2012
% holding as of December 31, 2012	25%	26.7%
Operating revenues	3,594	949
Operating income	(119)	11
Net income / loss	(280)	14
Stockholders' equity	201	203
Total assets	**2,634**	**681**
Total liabilities and stockholders' equity	**2,634**	**681**
	12/31/2013	03/31/2013
% holding as of December 31, 2013		26.7%
Operating revenues		902
Operating income		(82)
Net income / loss		(72)
Stockholders' equity		281
Total assets		**1,104**
Total liabilities and stockholders' equity		**1,104**

Note 23 Pension assets

(In € million)	December 31, 2013	December 31, 2012 Pro forma	January 1, 2012 Pro forma
Opening balance	**2,477**	**2,336**	**2,995**
Net periodic pension (cost) / income for the period	(277)	(190)	(36)
Contributions paid to the funds	342	359	258
First application of IAS 19 Revised " Employee Benefits" (Note 2)	-	-	(881)
Fair value revaluation	(138)	(29)	-
Reclassification	-	1	-
Closing balance	**2,454**	**2,477**	**2,336**

The detail of these pension assets is presented in Note 31.1.

Note 24 Other financial assets

As of December 31 (In € million)	2013		2012	
	Current	Non current	Current	Non current
Financial assets available for sale				
Available shares	-	762	-	475
Shares secured	-	373	-	229
Assets at fair value through profit and loss				
Marketable securities	106	20	235	85
Cash secured	825	-	636	-
Loans and receivables				
Financial lease deposit (bonds)	12	142	31	125
Financial lease deposit (others)	65	560	11	639
Loans and receivables	23	125	20	124
Gross value	*1,031*	*1,982*	*933*	*1,677*
Impairment at opening date	-	*(12)*	-	*(11)*
New impairment charge	-	(7)	-	(11)
Use of provision	-	-	-	10
Impairment at closing date	-	*(19)*	-	*(12)*
Total	**1,031**	**1,963**	**933**	**1,665**

Financial assets available for sale are as follows:

(In € million)	Fair Value	% interest	Stockholder's equity	Net income	Stock price (in €)	Closing date
As of December 31, 2013						
Amadeus*	1,076	7.73%	ND**	ND**	31.10	December 2013
Alitalia	22	7.08%	ND**	ND**	NA***	December 2013
Other	37	-	-	-	-	-
Total	**1,135**					
As of December 31, 2012						
Amadeus*	659	7.73%	1,531	496	19.05	December 2012
Other	45	-	-	-	-	-
Total	**704**					

* Listed company.
** Non-available.
*** Non-applicable.

Assets at fair value through profit and loss mainly comprise shares in mutual funds that do not meet the "cash equivalents" definition and cash account secured, mainly within the framework of the swap contract with Natixis on the OCEANE 2005 *(see Note 32)* and the guarantee given to the European Union concerning the anti-trust litigation *(see Note 31)*.

Concerning the Amadeus shares, on November 13, 2012, the Group entered into a hedging transaction with Société Générale to hedge the value of one third of its stake, i.e 12 million shares. The hedging instrument implemented was a collar. As part of this transaction, a loan of the same number of shares was set up with Société Générale. The collar was qualified as a fair value hedge. Its fair value amounts to €108 million as of December 31, 2013 (against €0.2 million as of December 31, 2012).

Loans and receivables mainly include deposits on flight equipment made within the framework of operating and capital leases.

Transfer of financial assets that are not derecognized in their entirety

▐ *Transfer of receivables agreement*
The Group entered into a loan agreement secured by Air France's 1% housing loans. For each of the CILs (Comités interprofessionnels du logement), Air France and the bank concluded a tripartite receivables delegation agreement with reference to the loan agreement. Through this agreement, the CILs commit to repaying the bank directly on each payment date. These are imperfect delegations: in the event of non repayment by the CILs, Air France remains liable to the bank for the loan repayments and interest. As of December 31, 2013, the amount of transferred receivables stood at €111 million (against €112 million as of December 31, 2012). The associated loan stood at €81 million as of December 31, 2013 (against €80 million as of December 31, 2012).

▐ *Loan of shares agreement*
On November 13, 2012, the Group signed a loan of shares agreement on Amadeus shares, within the framework of the hedging transaction to protect the value of Amadeus shares, as described above. As of December 31, 2013, the amount of the loan, excluding hedge effect, amounts to €373 million (against €229 million as of December 31, 2012).

Transfer of financial assets that are derecognized in their entirety

Since 2011, the Group has established non recourse transfert agreements concerning trade passenger, cargo and airlines receivables.

These agreements apply to receivables originating in France and other European countries for a total transferred amount of €211 million as of December 31, 2013, against €246 million as of December 31, 2012.

As of December 31, 2013, the link retained by the Group with the transferred assets represents a risk of dilution for which guarantee funds have been secured for €10 million, against €9 million as of December 31, 2012.

End of December 2013, the Group concluded a contract with a bank transfer without recourse by way of discount on the entire Receivable Tax Credit for Competitiveness Employment (CICE) 2013 with a notional amount of €42 million. The contract of assignment transferring substantially all the risks and rewards of the debt to the bank, the debt has been fully derecognised. As of December 31, 2013 the Group has a receivable from the bank corresponding to 5% of the nominal value of the assigned receivable, payable when the specific CICE statement will be sent to the tax administration in 2014.

Note 25 Inventories

As of December 31 (In € million)	2013	2012
Aeronautical spare parts	510	508
Other supplies	158	176
Production work in progress	7	7
Gross value	*675*	*691*
Opening valuation allowance	*(170)*	*(173)*
Charge to allowance	(11)	(18)
Use of allowance	11	18
Releases of allowance no longer required	-	-
Reclassification	6	3
Closing valuation allowance	*(164)*	*(170)*
Net value of inventory	*511*	*521*

Note 26 Trade accounts receivables

As of December 31 (In € million)	2013	2012
Airlines	399	495
Other clients:		
♦ Passenger	681	625
♦ Cargo	353	378
♦ Maintenance	377	364
♦ Other	52	82
Gross value	*1,862*	*1,944*
Opening valuation allowance	*(85)*	*(88)*
Charge to allowance	(21)	(18)
Use of allowance	16	19
Change of scope	2	-
Reclassification	1	2
Closing valuation allowance	*(87)*	*(85)*
Net value	*1,775*	*1,859*

Note 27 Other assets

As of December 31 (In € million)	2013		2012	
	Current	Non current	Current	Non current
Suppliers with debit balances	140	-	161	-
State receivable	72	-	71	-
Derivative instruments	267	97	201	103
Prepaid expenses	164	16	156	49
Other debtors	181	-	241	-
Gross value	*824*	*113*	*830*	*152*
Opening valuation allowance	*(2)*	*-*	*(2)*	*-*
Charge to allowance	(1)	-	-	-
Use of allowance	1	-	-	-
Closing valuation allowance	**(2)**	**-**	**(2)**	**-**
Net realizable value of other assets	*822*	*113*	*828*	*152*

As of December 31, 2012, non-current derivatives comprised an amount of €9 million relating to currency hedges on financial debt.

Note 28 Cash, cash equivalents and bank overdrafts

As of December 31 (In € million)	2013	2012
Liquidity funds (SICAV) (assets at fair value through profit and loss)	1,563	2,467
Bank deposits and term accounts (assets at fair value through profit and loss)	1,141	334
Cash in hand	980	619
Total cash and cash equivalents	*3,684*	*3,420*
Bank overdrafts	(166)	(257)
Cash, cash equivalents and bank overdrafts	*3,518*	*3,163*

The Group holds €3,684 million in cash as of December 31, 2013, including €199 million placed on bank accounts in Venezuela. This amount comes from the sale of airline tickets made locally during the period from December 2012 to December 2013. Under the exchange control, monthly requests for money transfers have been made to the Commission of Currency Administration (Comisión de Administración de-Divisas - CADIVI). Given the economic and political context of Venezuela, these requests did not give rise to currency transfers (the last transfer tooking place in October 2013).

Note 29 Equity attributable to equity holders of Air France-KLM SA

29.1 Issued capital

As of December 31, 2013, the issued capital of Air France-KLM comprised 300,219,278 fully paid-up shares. Each share with a nominal value of one euro is entitled to one vote.

The change in the number of issued shares is as follows:

As of December 31 (In number of shares)	2013	2012
At the beginning of the period	*300,219,278*	*300,219,278*
Issuance of shares for OCEANE conversion	-	-
At the end of the period	*300,219,278*	*300,219,278*
Of which:		
◆ number of shares issued and paid up	300,219,278	300,219,278
◆ number of shares issued and not paid up	-	-

The shares comprising the issued capital of Air France-KLM are subject to no restriction or priority concerning dividend distribution or reimbursement of the issued capital.

Authorized stock

The Combined Ordinary and Extraordinary Shareholders' Meeting of May 16, 2013 authorized the Board of Directors, for a period of 26 months from the date of the Meeting, to issue shares and/or other securities conferring immediate or future rights to Air France-KLM's capital limited to a total maximum nominal amount of €120 million.

Breakdown of the share capital and voting rights

The breakdown of the share capital and voting rights is as follows:

	% of capital		% of voting rights	
As of December 31	2013	2012	2013	2012
French State	16%	16%	16%	16%
Employees and former employees	7%	10%	7%	10%
Treasury shares	1%	1%	-	-
Other	76%	73%	77%	74%
Total	**100%**	**100%**	**100%**	**100%**

The item "Employees and former employees" includes shares held by employees and former employees identified in funds or by a Sicovam code.

Other securities giving access to common stock

▌ *OCEANE*
See Note 32.2.

29.2 Additional paid-in capital

Additional paid-in capital represents the difference between the nominal value of equity securities issued and the value of contributions in cash or in kind received by Air France-KLM.

29.3 Treasury shares

	Treasury shares	
	Number	**(In € million)**
December 31, 2011	*5,639,477*	*(89)*
Change in the period	(1,450,072)	4
December 31, 2012	*4,189 405*	*(85)*
Change in the period	(9,601)	-
December 31, 2013	*4,179,804*	*(85)*

As of December 31, 2013, Air France-KLM held 3,063,384 of its own shares acquired pursuant to the annual authorizations granted by the Shareholders' Meeting. As of December 31, 2013, the Group also held 1,116,420 of its own shares in respect of KLM stock option programs. All these treasury shares are classified as a reduction of equity.

29.4 Reserves and retained earnings

(In € million)	December 31, 2013	December 31, 2012 Pro forma	January 1, 2012 Pro forma
Legal reserve	70	70	70
Distributable reserves	734	850	962
Pension defined benefit reserves	(1,193)	(1,203)	(1,083)
Derivatives reserves	(47)	(43)	55
Available for sale securities reserves	655	253	86
Other reserves	664	1,701	2,127
Net income (loss) – Group share	(1,827)	(1,225)	(442)
Total	**(944)**	**403**	**1,775**

As of December 31, 2013, the legal reserve of €70 million represented 23% of Air France-KLM's issued capital. French company law requires that a limited company *(société anonyme)* allocates 5% of its unconsolidated statutory net income each year to this legal reserve until it reaches 10% of the Group's issued capital. The amount allocated to this legal reserve is deducted from the distributable income for the current year.

The legal reserve of any company subject to this requirement may only be distributed to shareholders upon liquidation of the company.

Note 30 Share-based compensation

30.1 Outstanding share-based compensation plans and other plans as of December 31, 2013

As of December 31, 2013, there were no outstanding share-based compensation plans in the Air France-KLM Group.

Changes in options

	Average exercise price (€)	Number of options
Options outstanding as of December 31, 2011	34.21	390,517
Of which: options exercisable at December 31, 2011	34.21	390,517
Options forfeited during the period	34.21	(390,517)
Options exercised during the period	-	-
Options granted during the period	-	-
Options outstanding as of December 31, 2012	-	-
Of which: options exercisable at December 31, 2012	-	-
Options forfeited during the period	-	
Options exercised during the period	-	
Options granted during the period	-	
Options outstanding as of December 31, 2013	-	-
Of which: options exercisable at December 31, 2013	-	-

Description of KLM stock-option plans

Prior to the combination with Air France, members of the Management Board and the key executives of KLM had been granted KLM stock options. Within the combination agreement between KLM and Air France, stock-options and SAR (Share Appreciation Rights) that were not exercised during the operation were modified on May 4, 2004 so that their holders could purchase Air France-KLM shares and SARs attached to Air France-KLM shares. The shares held by

KLM within this plan were converted into Air France-KLM shares and transferred to a foundation whose sole purpose is their retention until the stock options are exercised or forfeited.

The vesting conditions of the stock-option plan granted by KLM in July 2007 are such that one third of the options vest at grant date with a further one third after one and two years, respectively. Vesting was conditional on KLM achieving predetermined non-market-dependent performance criteria.

30.2 KLM PPSs plan

During the periods ending December 31, 2013 and December 31, 2012, cash-settled share-based compensation plans index-linked to the change in the Air France-KLM share price were granted by KLM. They correspond to share-based plans with settlement in cash (PPS).

Plans	Grant date	Number of PPSs granted	Start date for PPSs exercise	Date of expiry	Number of PPSs exercised as of 12/31/2013
KLM	01/07/2008	153,080	01/07/2008	01/07/2013	68,451
KLM	01/07/2009	136,569	01/07/2009	01/07/2014	23,615
KLM	01/07/2010	145,450	01/07/2010	01/07/2015	12,189
KLM	01/07/2011	144,235	01/07/2011	01/07/2016	-
KLM	01/04/2012	146,004	01/04/2012	01/04/2017	-
KLM	01/04/2013	150,031	01/04/2013	01/04/2018	-

The changes in PPSs were as follows:

	Number of PPSs
PPSs outstanding as of December 31, 2011	**465,497**
Of which: SARs exercisable at December 31, 2011	*270,908*
PPSs granted during the period	146,004
PPSs exercised during the period	(51,348)
PPSs forfeited during the period	13,493
PPSs outstanding as of December 31, 2012	**573,646**
Of which: PPSs exercisable at December 31, 2012	*357,687*
PPSs granted during the period	150,031
PPSs exercised during the period	(104,255)
PPSs forfeited during the period	(99,064)
PPSs outstanding as of December 31, 2013	**520,358**
Of which: PPSs exercisable at December 31, 2013	*330,807*

The vesting conditions of the PPSs plans granted by KLM are such that one third of the options vest at grant date, with a further one third after one and two years, respectively. Vesting is conditional on KLM achieving predetermined non-market-dependent performance criteria.

The fair value of the services provided under the PPSs plan has been determined according to the market value of the Air France-KLM share at the closing date i.e €7.58:

PPSs	Fair value as of December 31, 2013 (In € million)
01/07/2009	0.4
01/07/2010	0.6
01/07/2011	0.9
01/04/2012	0.9
01/04/2013	1.1

30.3 Salary expenses related to share-based compensation

Period from January 1 to December 31	2013	2012
(In € million)		
2005 Shares-for-Salary Exchange	2	3
Stock option plan	1	2
Salary expenses (Note 8)	**3**	**5**

Note 31 Provisions and retirement benefits

(In € million)	Retirement benefits Note 31.1	Restitution of aircraft	Restructuring	Litigation	Others	Total
Amount as of January 1, 2012 (pro forma)	**1,687**	**575**	**12**	**404**	**170**	**2,848**
Of which:						
♦ Non-current	1,687	459	-	390	156	2,692
♦ Current	-	116	12	14	14	156
New provision	84	259	442	51	103	**939**
Use of provision	(91)	(119)	(26)	(15)	(39)	**(290)**
Reversal of unnecessary provisions	-	(3)	-	(1)	-	**(4)**
Fair value revaluation	283	-	-	-	-	**283**
Currency translation adjustment	1	1	-	-	1	**3**
Discount/Accretion impact	-	(25)	-	-	-	**(25)**
Reclassification	1	(47)	-	-	5	**(41)**
Amount as of December 31, 2012 (pro forma)	**1,965**	**641**	**428**	**439**	**240**	**3,713**
Of which:						
♦ Non-current	1,965	545	4	429	215	3,158
♦ Current	-	96	424	10	25	555
New provision	99	272	282	76	97	**826**
Use of provision	(39)	(123)	(233)	(43)	(79)	**(517)**
Reversal of unnecessary provisions	-	(18)	(34)	-	(6)	**(58)**
Fair value revaluation	(162)	-	-	-	-	**(162)**
Currency translation adjustment	(9)	(1)	-	-	(1)	**(11)**
Change in scope	2	-	-	-	(2)	**-**
Discount/Accretion impact	-	(2)	-	-	-	**(2)**
Reclassification	(3)	(15)	(1)	2	-	**(17)**
Amount as of December 31, 2013	**1,853**	**754**	**442**	**474**	**249**	**3,772**
Of which:						
♦ Non-current	1,853	606	-	439	204	3,102
♦ Current	-	148	442	35	45	670

As of December 31, 2013, the impact on the net periodic pension cost, amounting to €54 million, linked to the restructuring plans of Air France and its regional subsidiaries has been recorded in "Other non-current income and expenses" *(see Note 11)*.

As of December 31, 2012, the impact was about €81 million and was also recorded in "Other non-current income and expenses".

Movements in provisions for restructuring which have an impact on the income statement are recorded in "other non-current income and expenses" when the plans concerned have a material impact *(see Note 11)*.

Movements in provisions for restitution of aircraft which have an impact on the income statement are recorded in "provisions" except

for the discount/accretion impact which is recorded in "other financial income and expenses".

Movements in provisions for litigation and in provisions for other risks and charges which have an impact on the income statement are recorded, depending on their nature, in the different lines of the income statement.

31.1 Retirement benefits

The Group has a large number of retirement and other long-term benefits plans for its employees, several of which are defined benefit plans. The specific characteristics (benefit formulas, funding policies and types of assets held) of the plans vary according to the regulations and laws in the particular country in which the employees are located. As indicated in Notes 2 and 4, since January 1, 2013, the Group has applied the standard IAS 19 Revised "Employee benefits". To facilitate comparison, the financial statements as of December 31, 2012 have been restated in accordance with the new rules.

31.1.1 Characteristics of the main defined benefit plans

▌ *Pension plan related to flight deck crew - Netherlands*
The pension plan related to the flight deck crew in the KLM entity is a defined benefit plan with a reversion to the spouse on the beneficiary's death.

The retirement age defined in the plan is 56 years.

The Board of the pension fund comprises members appointed by the employer and employees and has full responsibility for the administration and management of the plan. KLM can only control the financing agreement between KLM and the pension fund. The financing agreement is part of the Collective Labor Agreement between KLM and the Unions/Works Council.

To satisfy the requirements of the Dutch regulations and the agreements defined between the employer and the pension fund Board, the plan has a minimum mandatory funding ratio of 105% of the projected short-term obligation, and approximately 115% to 120% of the projected long-term obligation. The projection of these commitments is calculated based on the local funding rules.

If the coverage ratio is under the funding agreement detailed above, the company is required to make additional contributions: within the current year for non-compliance with the 105% threshold or within 10 years for non-compliance with the 115% to 120% threshold. The amount of normal and additional employer contributions is not limited. The employee contributions cannot be increased in the event of non-compliance with these minimum funding rules.

A reduction in the employer contribution is possible if the indexation of pensions is fully funded. This reduction is not capped and can be realised either via a reimbursement of contributions, or by a reduction in future contributions.

The return on plan assets, the discount rate used to value the obligations and the longevity and characteristics of the active population are the main factors liable to influence the coverage ratio and lead to a risk of additional contributions for KLM.

The funds, which are fully dedicated to the KLM Group companies, are mainly invested in bonds, equities and real estate.

The management of most assets is outsourced to a private institution, under a service contract.

The required funding of this pension plan also includes a buffer against the following risks: interest rate risks, equity risks, currency risks, credit risks, actuarial risks and real estate risks.

For example, about 90% of the currency risk is hedged. Put options are in place, which cover a decrease of about 25% of the value of the equity portfolio.

▌ *Pension plan related to ground staff - Netherlands*
The pension plan related to the ground staff in the KLM entity is a defined benefit plan with a reversion to the spouse on the beneficiary's death.

The retirement age defined in the plan was 65 years until December 31, 2013 and 67 years after this date.

The Board of the pension fund comprises members appointed by the employer and employees and has full responsibility for the administration and management of the plan. KLM can only control the financing agreement between KLM and the pension fund. The financing agreement is part of the Collective Labor Agreement between KLM and the Unions/Works Council.

To satisfy the requirements of Dutch regulations and the agreements defined between the employer and the pension fund Board, the plan has a minimum mandatory funding ratio of 105% of the projected short-term obligation, and approximately 115% to 120% of the projected long-term obligation. The projection of these commitments is calculated based on the local funding rules.

If the coverage ratio is under the funding agreement detailed above, the company and the employee are required to make additional contributions: within the current year for non-compliance with the 105% threshold or within 15 years for non-compliance with the 115% to 120% threshold. The amount of basic and additional employer contributions is not limited. Any additional employee contributions are limited to 2% of the pension basis.

A reduction in contributions is possible if the indexation of pensions is fully funded. This reduction is not capped and can be realised either via a reimbursement of contributions, or by a reduction in future contributions.

The return on plan assets, the discount rate used to value the obligations and the longevity and characteristics of the active population are the main factors liable to both influence the coverage ratio and the level of the normal contribution for future pension accrual. The normal contributions are limited to 24% of the pension base.

The funds, which are fully dedicated to the KLM Group companies, are mainly invested in bonds, equities and real estate. The management of most assets is outsourced to a private institution, under a service contract.

The required funding of this pension plan also includes a buffer against the following risks: interest rate risks, equity risks, currency risks, credit risks, actuarial risks and real estate risks. For example, an interest hedge is foreseen to halve the potential impact of the sensitivity to an interest rate decrease. Similarly, about 90% of the currency risk is hedged. Put options are in place, which cover a decrease of about 25% of the value of the equity portfolio.

Pension plan related to cabin crew - Netherlands

The pension plan related to the cabin crew in the KLM entity is a defined benefit plan with a reversion to the spouse on the beneficiary's death.

The pension is calculated based on their final salaries for employees hired since 2009, and based on average salaries for their entire careers for the other employees.

The retirement age defined in the plan is 60 years.

The Board of the pension fund comprises members appointed by the employer and employees and has full responsibility for the administration and management of the plan. KLM can only control the financing agreement between KLM and the pension fund. The financing agreement is part of the Collective Labor Agreement between KLM and the Unions/Works Council.

To satisfy the requirements of Dutch regulations and the agreements defined between the employer and the pension fund Board, the plan has a minimum mandatory funding ratio of 105% of the projected short-term obligation, and approximately 115% to 120% of the projected long-term obligation. The projection of these commitments is calculated based on the local funding rules.

If the coverage ratio is under the funding agreement detailed above, the company and the employee have to pay additional contributions: within three years for non-compliance with the 105% threshold or within 15 years for non-compliance with the 115% to 120% threshold. The amount of normal and additional employer contributions is capped at 48% of the pension basis. Any additional employee contributions are limited to 0.7% of the pension basis.

A reduction in contributions is possible if the indexation of pensions is fully funded. This reduction is limited to twice the normal annual contribution.

The return on plan assets, the discount rate used to value the obligations and the longevity and characteristics of the active population are the main factors liable to both influence the coverage ratio and the level of the normal contribution for future pension accrual.

The funds, which are fully dedicated to the KLM Group companies, are mainly invested in bonds, equities and real estate. The management of most assets is outsourced to a private institution, under a service contract.

The required funding of this pension plan also includes a buffer against the following risks: interest rate risks, equity risks, currency risks, credit risks, actuarial risks and real estate risks.

For example, an interest hedge is foreseen to halve the potential impact of the sensitivity to an interest rate decrease.

Similarly, about 90% of the currency risk is hedged. Put options are in place, which cover a decrease of about 25% of the value of the equity portfolio.

Air France pension plan (CRAF) – France

The employees covered by this plan are the Air France ground staff affiliated to the CRAF until December 31, 1992. The participants receive, or will receive on retirement, an additional pension paid monthly and permanently calculated based on the data known as of December 31, 1992 and expressed in the form of points. The value of each point is reevaluated every year based on the weighted increases seen in the CNAV and ARRCO schemes over the last twelve months.

Until 2009, the CRAF had the legal form of a supplementary pension institution (pursuant to the "Sécurité sociale" Code). With this status, the CRAF was responsible, on behalf of the Air France ground staff employed in France, for managing the pension plan resulting from the merging of the Air France ground staff plan with the mandatory pension plan for the private sector.

Following the 2003 law on pension reform, foreseeing the disappearance of supplementary pension institutions as of December 31, 2008, the CRAF's Board of Directors opted to transform it into an institution managing supplementary pensions. The CRAF is now responsible for the administrative functions linked to the plan. The pension rights were not amended by this reform. Air France is directly responsible for the pension obligations.

As of December 31, 2008, all the funds managed by the CRAF had been transferred to two insurance companies. On December 31, 2012, one of the insurance contracts was terminated and its funds were transferred to the other, which thus became the only insurer.

This insurance company guarantees a capital equal to the amount of capital invested in units of account in its collective fund, which represents a little more than 5% of the amount of funds, this percentage being automatically set to increase over time.

The annual payments made by Air France to the insurance company are governed by the agreement signed with the employee representative bodies on December 14, 2009. The minimum annual payment defined by this agreement amounts to €32.5 million. If the value of the funds falls below 50% of the total obligations calculated for funding purposes, Air France is required to make an additional payment to achieve a minimum 50% coverage rate.

The funds are invested in bonds, equities and general assets of the insurance company. Studies of assets/liabilities allocation are carried out regularly, to verify the relevance of the investment strategy.

Air France end of service benefit plan (ICS) - France

Pursuant to French regulations and the company agreements, every employee receives an end of service indemnity when leaving the company for retirement.

In France, this indemnity depends on the number of years of service, the professional category of the employee (flight deck crew, cabin crew, ground staff, agent, technician and executive) and, in some cases, on the age of the employee at retirement.

On retirement, employees consequently receive an end of service indemnity based on their final salaries over the last twelve-months and on their seniority.

The indemnity is only payable to employees on their retirement date.

There is no mandatory minimum funding requirement for this scheme.

Air France has nevertheless signed contracts with three insurance companies to pre-finance the plan. The company has sole responsibility for payment of the indemnities, but remains free to make payments to the insurance companies.

The relevant outsourced funds are invested in bonds and equities.

As of December 31, 2013, the three Dutch plans and the two French plans presented above represent a respective 79% and 12% of the Group's pension liabilities and 91% and 4% of the Group's pension assets.

31.1.2 Description of the actuarial assumptions and related sensitivities

Actuarial valuations of the Group's benefit obligation have been made as of December 31, 2013 and December 31, 2012. These calculations include:

- assumptions on staff turnover and life expectancy of the beneficiaries of the plan;
- assumptions on salary and pension increases;
- assumptions of retirement ages varying from 55 to 67 depending on the localization and the applicable laws;
- discount rates used to determine the actuarial present value of the projected benefit obligations.

The discount rates for the different geographical areas are thus determined based on the duration of each plans, taking into account the average trend in interest rates on high quality bonds, observed on the main available indices. In some countries, where the market regarding this type of bond is not broad enough, the discount rate is determined with reference to government bonds. Most of the Group's benefit obligations are located in the Euro zone, where the discount rates used are as follows:

As of December 31	2013	2012
Euro zone - Duration 10 to 15 years	3.00%	3.00%
Euro zone - Duration 15 years and more	3.65%	3.65%

The duration between 10 and 15 years mainly concerns the plans located in France while the duration of 15 years and beyond mainly concerns plans located in the Netherlands.

On an average basis, the main assumptions used to value the liabilities are summarized below:

- the rate of salary increase (excluding inflation) is 1.75% for the Group as of December 31, 2013 against 1.69% as of December 31, 2012;

- the rate of pension increase (excluding inflation) is 1.36% for the Group as of December 31, 2013 against 1.46% as of December 31, 2012.

The sensitivity of the pension obligations to a change in assumptions, based on actuarial calculations, is as follows:

➤ Sensitivity to changes in the discount rate

(In € million)	Sensitivity of the assumptions for the year ended December 31, 2013	Sensitivity of the assumptions for the year ended December 31, 2012 (pro forma)
0.25% increase in the discount rate	(688)	(667)
0.25% decrease in the discount rate	792	825

➤ Sensitivity to changes in salary increase

(In € million)	Sensitivity of the assumptions for the year ended December 31, 2013	Sensitivity of the assumptions for the year ended December 31, 2012 (pro forma)
0.25% increase in the salary increase rate	142	146
0.25% decrease in the salary increase rate	(127)	(133)

➤ Sensitivity to changes in pension increase

(In € million)	Sensitivity of the assumptions for the year ended December 31, 2013	Sensitivity of the assumptions for the year ended December 31, 2012 (pro forma)
0.25% increase in the pension increase rate	629	505
0.25% decrease in the pension increase rate	(538)	(489)

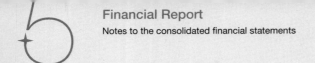

31.1.3 Evolution of commitments

The following table details the reconciliation between the benefits obligation and plan assets of the Group and the amounts recorded in the financial statements for the years ended December 31, 2013 and December 31, 2012 (pro forma).

(In € million)	As of December 31, 2013			As of December 31, 2012		
	Netherlands	France	Others	Netherlands	France	Others
Benefit obligation at beginning of year	**13,258**	**2,191**	**870**	**11,411**	**2,016**	**706**
Service cost	386	65	13	340	53	21
Interest cost	478	64	31	556	94	34
Employees' contribution	45	-	1	54	-	1
Plan amendments and curtailment	(41)	(56)	(5)	-	(82)	(3)
Change in consolidation scope	-	2	-	-	-	-
Benefits paid	(383)	(101)	(28)	(360)	(114)	(39)
Transfers of assets/liability through balance sheet	2	(5)	-	-	-	-
Actuarial loss / (gain) demographic assumptions	(16)	(3)	(1)	103	-	-
Actuarial loss / (gain) financial assumptions	(203)	(25)	(43)	1,193	247	136
Actuarial loss / (gain) experience gap	133	(16)	(6)	(22)	(23)	4
Currency translation adjustment	10	-	(35)	-	-	11
Other	-	-	-	(17)	-	(1)
Benefit obligation at end of year	**13,669**	**2,116**	**797**	**13,258**	**2,191**	**870**
Including benefit obligation resulting from schemes totally or partly funded	*13,575*	*2,055*	*690*	*13,167*	*2,131*	*729*
Including unfunded benefit obligation	*94*	*61*	*107*	*91*	*60*	*141*
Fair value of plan assets at beginning of year	**15,528**	**787**	**515**	**13,563**	**768**	**450**
Actual return on plan assets	346	71	38	1,904	96	60
Employers' contributions	361	(11)	14	384	37	2
Employees' contributions	45	-	1	54	-	1
Change in consolidation scope	(1)	-	1	-	-	-
Settlements	-	-	(1)	-	-	-
Transfers of assets/liability through balance sheet	-	-	-	-	-	1
Benefits paid	(375)	(99)	(21)	(360)	(114)	(8)
Currency translation adjustment	(1)	-	(15)	-	-	10
Other	-	-	-	(17)	-	(1)
Fair value of plan assets at end of year	**15,903**	**748**	**532**	**15,528**	**787**	**515**

(In € million)	As of December 31, 2013			As of December 31, 2012		
	Netherlands	**France**	**Others**	**Netherlands**	**France**	**Others**
Amounts recorded in the balance sheet*:						
Pension asset (Note 23)	2,452	-	2	2,477	-	-
Provision for retirement benefits	(220)	(1,368)	(265)	(207)	(1,404)	(354)
Net amount recognized	*2,232*	*(1,368)*	*(263)*	*2,270*	*(1,404)*	*(354)*
Net periodic cost:						
Service cost	386	65	13	340	53	21
Interest cost	(90)	41	12	(123)	59	11
Plan amendments and curtailment	(40)	(57)	(5)	-	(82)	(1)
Settlement	-	-	1	-	-	-
Net periodic cost	**256**	**49**	**21**	**217**	**30**	**31**

* *All the obligations are recorded as non-current liabilities, except for the pension plans for which the balance is a net asset fully recorded as a non-current asset.*

▌ *Amendments and curtailment of pension plans*

As of December 31, 2013, a curtailment has been booked by Air France and its subsidiaries for an amount of €54 million, relating to the voluntary departure plan *(see Note 11)*.

By KLM, the amendments of pension plans led to a decrease of €40 million of the defined benefit obligation: €25 million further to the modification of the retirement age from 65 to 67 years concerning the ground staff pension plan and €15 million further to the decrease of the annual accrual rates on cabin crew and ground staff pension plans.

As of December 31, 2012, a curtailment was booked by Air France and its subsidiaries for an amount of €81 million, relating to the voluntary departure plan *(see Note 11)*.

31.1.4 Asset allocation

The weighted average allocation of the funds invested in the Group's pension and other long-term benefit plans is as follows:

Funds invested	As of December 31, 2013		As of December 31, 2012	
	France	**Netherlands**	**France**	**Netherlands**
Equities	41%	38%	40%	38%
Bonds	46%	50%	49%	51%
Real estate	-	10%	-	10%
Others	13%	2%	11%	1%
Total	**100%**	**100%**	**100%**	**100%**

Equities are mainly invested in active markets in Europe, United States and emerging countries.

Bonds are primarily composed of government bonds, at least rated BBB, and invested in Europe, United States and emerging countries.

Real estate assets are mainly located in Europe and in the United States.

The Group's pension assets do not include assets occupied or used by the Group.

31.1.5 Expected cash flows and risks linked to the pension obligations

The expected cash flows relative to the defined benefit pension plans will amount to €435 million for the year ending as of December 31, 2014. The weighted average duration of the obligation is 18 years.

The funding, capitalization and matching strategies implemented by the Group are presented in paragraph 30.1.

According to this description, the Group has no obligation to recapitalize the plans for which a minimum funding is required over the short or long term.

31.2   Provisions for restructuring

As of December 31, 2013 and December 31, 2012, provision for restructuring mainly includes the provision for the voluntary departure plans of Air France and its regional affiliates *(see Note 11)*.

31.3   Provisions for litigation

31.3.1 Provision for litigation with third parties

An assessment of litigation risks with third parties was carried out with the Group's attorneys and provisions have been recorded whenever circumstances required.

Provisions for litigation with third parties also include provisions for tax risks. Such provisions are set up when the Group considers that the tax authorities could challenge a tax position adopted by the Group or one of its subsidiaries.

In the normal course of its activities, the Air France-KLM Group and its subsidiaries Air France and KLM (and their subsidiaries) are involved in litigation, some of which may be significant.

31.3.2 Provision for litigation concerning anti-trust laws in the air-freight industry

Air France, KLM and Martinair, a wholly-owned subsidiary of KLM since January 1, 2009, have been involved, since February 2006, with up to twenty-five other airlines in investigations initiated by the anti-trust authorities in several countries, with respect to allegations of anti-competitive agreements or concerted actions in the air-freight industry.

As of December 31, 2013 most of these proceedings had resulted in Plea Agreements made by Air France, KLM and Martinair with the appropriate agencies, and the payment of settlement amounts which ended procedures.

In Europe, the European Commission announced, on November 9, 2010, its decision to impose fines on 14 airlines including Air France, KLM and Martinair related to anti-competition practices - mainly concerning fuel surcharges in the air freight industry. The Commission imposed an overall fine of €340 million on the Air France-KLM Group companies.

As the Group's parent company, Air France-KLM was considered by the European Commission to be jointly and severally liable for the anti-competitive practices of which the Group companies were found guilty.

On January 24 and 25, 2011, the Group companies filed an appeal against the decision before the General Court of the European Union.

Since the appeal does not suspend the payment of the fines, the Group companies chose not to pay the fine immediately, but to provide bank guarantees until a definitive ruling by the European Courts.

On January 10, 2014 the Swiss anti-trust authority (COMCO) imposed a fine of €3.2 million on Air France and KLM. The Group companies intend to file an appeal on this decision before the Federal Administrative Tribunal.

In South Korea on November 29, 2010, the Korean antitrust authority (KFTC) imposed on Air France-KLM, Air France and KLM a total fine of €8.8 million which was paid in January 2011. The Group companies filed an appeal before the competent Seoul High Court in December 2010.

On May 16, 2012 the 6th chamber of the Seoul High Court vacated the KFTC's decision against Air France-KLM on the grounds that Air France-KLM was not engaged in the air freight transportation business after it converted to a holding company on September 15, 2004. With regard to the appeals of Air France and KLM, the Court found in favour of the KFTC. Appeal filings against the Court decisions were submitted to the Supreme Court by both Air France and KLM in June 2012. Generally, the Supreme Court appeal process will take 1-2 years to conclude.

Since January 10, 2014 (the imposition of a fine by the Swiss antitrust authorities), the Group companies have no longer been exposed to anti-trust proceedings with respect to alleged of concerted actions in the air freight industry.

As of December 31, 2013, the total amount of provisions amounts to €372 million in respect of all the proceedings which have not yet been concluded by a final decision.

31.3.3 Other provisions

Other provisions are mainly provisions for power-by-hour contracts (maintenance activity of the Group), provisions for onerous leases, provisions for the portion of CO_2 emissions not covered by the free allocation of quotas and provisions for the dismantling of buildings.

31.4   Contingent liabilities

The Group is involved in a number of governmental, legal and arbitrage procedures for which provisions have not been recorded in the financial statements.

31.4.1 Litigations concerning anti-trust laws in the air-freight industry

These litigations have not been provisioned given that the Group is unable, given the current status of proceedings, to evaluate its exposure.

Pursuant to the initiation in February 2006 of the various competition authority investigations, class actions were brought by forwarding agents and air-freight shippers in several countries against Air France, KLM and Martinair, and the other freight carriers. In addition, civil suits have been filed in Europe by shippers following the European Commission's decision of November 9, 2010. The Group companies vigorously oppose all such civil actions.

▌ *United States*

In the United States, the Group concluded a Settlement Agreement with the representatives of the class action in July 2010, bringing to an end all claims and, court proceedings in connection with unlawful practices for cargo transportation to, from and within the United States.

With respect to those Air France, KLM and Martinair customers who chose to be excluded, a portion of the settlement proportional to the revenue Air France, KLM and Martinair received from those parties over the relevant period as compared with the overall revenue for this same period has been segregated in a separate escrow account. The parties who opted out are free to sue Air France, KLM and Martinair individually.

▌ Netherlands

a) Litigation vehicle Equilib has initiated two largely overlapping proceedings before the Amsterdam District Court aimed at establishing liability on behalf of 184 groups, whereby the actual amounts are to be determined in follow-up proceedings. Following the annulment by the Amsterdam Court of Appeal of the interim decision of the District Court to stay the proceedings, Air France, KLM and Martinair are due to file their statement of defence on April 2, 2014 in the first proceeding. The second proceeding will be introduced during the second half of 2014.

Air France, KLM and Martinair initiated contribution proceedings before the Amsterdam District Court against the other airlines included in the European Commission decision, which were stayed with the main proceedings. As the annulment of this stay by the Amsterdam Court of Appeal did not affect the stay of the contribution proceedings, Air France, KLM and Martinair asked the Court of Appeal in a separate appeal to annul the stay of the contribution proceedings, which would again synchronize the main and contribution proceedings.

b) A second litigation vehicle, East West Debt ("EWD"), also initiated proceedings before the Amsterdam District Court to obtain compensation from the Group, as well as two other European airlines, for the claims of 8 individual shippers. Following the annulment by the Amsterdam Court of Appeal of the interim decision of the District Court to stay the proceedings, the case is expected to resume at the District Court where a date will be set for filing the statement of defence.

The Group has also initiated contribution proceedings at the Amsterdam District Court against the other airlines included in the decision.

c) A third litigation vehicle Stichting Cartel Compensation ("SCC") initiated proceedings before the Amsterdam District Court to obtain compensation from the Goup and several other European and Asian airlines, for the claims of 877 individual shippers. The proceedings will be introduced on April 2, 2014.

▌ United Kingdom

In the United Kingdom, a civil suit has been filed against British Airways with the competent court by two flower importers.

British Airways issued contribution proceedings against all the airlines fined by the European Commission including entities of the Group. To date, British Airways has neither quantified nor substantiated its purported claims. These contribution proceedings have been stayed.

In the main proceedings, the plaintiffs were granted permission to add parties to the proceedings, resulting in over 500 plaintiffs.

▌ Australia

Within the context of ongoing class action proceedings instituted in 2007 against seven airlines (excluding the Air France-KLM Group) in the Australian Federal Court, cross claims have been filed against Air France, KLM and Martinair by Singapore Airlines (August 15, 2011), Cathay Pacific (August 15, 2011), Lufthansa (November 4, 2011), Air New Zealand (December 5, 2011) and British Airways (December 19, 2011). In the cross claims, the respondent airlines claim that if, despite their denial of the claims of wrongdoing in the class action, they are ordered to pay damages, they will seek contributions from the cross respondents. The Group companies have filed defences to these cross claims in which they deny that the respondent airlines are entitled to any contribution from them. As of December 31, 2013 this proceeding was still pending.

▌ Norway

On May 25, 2012, a civil suit was filed by a company named Marine Harvest before the Norwegian court on the grounds of allegedly additional costs caused by anti-competitive practices. The Group companies have requested a stay of the proceeding upon which the court has not ruled yet.

31.4.2 Legislation concerning anti-trust laws in the passenger sector

▌ Canada

A civil class action was reinitiated in 2013 by claimants in Ontario against seven airlines including Air France and KLM. The plaintiffs allege that the defendants participated in a conspiracy to increase the price of passenger services by an adjustment in fuel surcharges to and from Canada and on transatlantic destinations, for which they are claiming damages. Air France and KLM strongly deny any participation in such a conspiracy and intend to file a motion to dismiss.

31.4.3 Other litigations

a) Pretory

Company Air France, as a legal entity, was placed under investigation on July 20, 2006 on charges of concealed employment and as an accessory to misuse of corporate assets in connection with a judicial investigation initiated against the officers of Pretory, a company with which Air France, pursuant to the September 2001 attacks, had entered into an agreement for the provision of safety officers on certain flights. Despite a non prosecution decision by the Public Prosecutor, the investigating magistrate decided, on February 7, 2012, to bring the case to court on charges of concealed employment.

On July 9, 2013, the court imposed a €0.15 million fine on the company. Air France has filed an appeal against this decision which it deems to be without grounds.

b) KLM minority shareholders

On December 31, 2012, two KLM minority shareholders filed a request with the Enterprise Chamber of the Amsterdam Court of Appeal to order an enquiry into, amongst other matters, the KLM's dividend policy in respect of the years 2004-05 to 2010-11 periods. This file relates to a claim for higher dividend for the fiscal year 2007-08 by these shareholders together with the Vereniging van Effectenbezitters (VEB) initiated in January 2008 against KLM and Air France-KLM. In this last proceeding, a final decision ruling from the Dutch Supreme Court on July 2013 definitively rejected all claims against KLM.

The Enterprise Chamber did, however, uphold the request for an enquiry into the dividend policy for the period under consideration. The main focus of the enquiry is the manner in which Air France-KLM, in its capacity as the sole priority shareholder, and KLM's Management and Supervisory Boards executed clause 32 of KLM's Articles of Association. This provides that the priority shareholder may reserve part of the profits after consulting with the Management Board and the Supervisory Board of KLM.

c) Rio-Paris AF447 flight

Following to the crash of the Rio-Paris AF447 flight in the South Atlantic, a number of legal actions have been brought in the United States and Brazil and, more recently, in France by the victims' heirs.

All these proceedings are aimed at receiving damages as reparation for the losses suffered by the heirs of the passengers who died in the crash.

In the United States, all the proceedings have been consolidated in California before the Northern District Court.

On October 4, 2010, the District judge granted the defendants' motion for dismissal on grounds of "forum non convenience" and suggested that they pursue their claim in France.

On March 17 and 18, 2011 respectively, Airbus and Air France were indicted for manslaughter by the investigating magistrate and incur the penalties of fines prescribed by law. Air France intends to challenge its implication in this case.

These penalties should not have a material effect on the financial situation of Air France.

The damages as reparation for the losses suffered by the heirs of the passengers who died in the crash are covered by Air France's third-party liability insurance policy.

Except for the matters specified under the paragraphs 31.3, 31.4, the Group is not aware of any dispute or governmental, judicial and arbitration proceedings (including any proceedings of which the issuer is aware, or that are pending or threatened against it) that could have or have recently had a significant impact on the Group's financial position, earnings, assets, liabilities or profitability, during a period including at least the past twelve months.

Note 32 Financial debt

As of December 31 (In € million)	2013	2012
Non current financial debt		
Perpetual subordinated loan stock in Yen	211	256
Perpetual subordinated loan stock in Swiss francs	341	347
OCEANE (convertible bonds)	1,478	988
Bonds	1,200	1,950
Capital lease obligations	3,808	3,919
Other debt	1,558	2,105
Total	**8,596**	**9,565**
Current financial debt		
Bonds	741	-
Capital lease obligations	599	588
Other debt	653	734
Accrued interest	144	112
Total	**2,137**	**1,434**

32.1 Perpetual subordinated bond

32.1.1 Perpetual subordinated bond in Japanese Yen

The perpetual subordinated bond in Japanese Yen was issued by KLM in 1999 for a total amount of JPY 30 billion, i.e. €211 million as of December 31, 2013.

Until 2019, this perpetual subordinated bond is subject to the payment of a 5.28% coupon on a notional of USD 248 million.

The debt is perpetual. It is nevertheless reimbursable at its nominal value at the Group's discretion as of August 28, 2019. This reimbursement does not involve a premium. A premium would be due if the debt were to be reimbursed in a currency other than the yen.

This debt is subordinated to all other existing and future KLM debts.

32.1.2 Perpetual subordinated bond in Swiss francs

The perpetual subordinated bond in Swiss francs was issued by KLM in two installments in 1985 and 1986 for a total original amount of CHF 500 million. Following the purchases made by KLM, the outstanding subordinated bond amounts to CHF 419 million, i.e. €341 million as of December 31, 2013.

The bonds are reimbursable on certain dates at the Group's discretion at a price between nominal value and 101.25% (depending on the bond and date of early repayment).

This loan is subject to the payment of a coupon considered to be fixed-rate (5.75% on a CHF 270 million portion and 2.125% on a CHF 149 million portion) for the years ended December 31, 2013 and December 31, 2012.

This debt is subordinated to all other existing and future KLM debts.

32.2 OCEANE

32.2.1 OCEANE issued in 2005

In April 2005, the company Air France, a subsidiary of the Air France-KLM Group, issued convertible bonds maturing in 15 years. The conversion option allows for conversion and/or exchange at any time into new or existing Air France-KLM shares (OCEANE). 21,951,219 bonds were issued for a total amount of €450 million. Each bond has a nominal value of €20.50. As of December 31, 2013, the conversion ratio is 1.03 Air France-KLM shares for one bond.

The maturity date for this convertible bond is April 1, 2020. Bond holders could request reimbursement as of April 1, 2012 and will also be able to do this as of April 1, 2016. Air France holds a call option triggering early cash reimbursement which can be exercised starting April 1, 2010 and, under certain conditions, encouraging OCEANE holders to convert into Air France-KLM shares. The annual coupon is 2.75% payable in arrears at the end of each period ended April 1.

The conversion period of these bonds runs from June 1, 2005 to March 23, 2020, except in the event of early reimbursement.

On December 6, 2011, to optimize its debt repayment schedule by neutralizing the exercise of the OCEANE repayment option on April 1, 2012, Air France signed a swap agreement relating to these OCEANEs (total return swap) with Natixis expiring on April 1, 2016 at the latest. In order to hedge this contract, Natixis launched a contractual acquisition procedure to purchase the aforementioned OCEANEs.

This contract was thus reflected in the following operations:

+ the purchase by Natixis of 18,692,474 OCEANEs (i.e. 85.16% of the amount initially issued) at a fixed price of €21 following a contractual acquisition procedure open between December 7 and December 13, 2011. Natixis is the owner of the acquired OCEANEs and did not exercise its early repayment option on April 1, 2012;
+ the entry into force effective December 14, 2011 of a swap contract expiring on April 1, 2016 whose notional amounts to €392.5 million (number of OCEANEs acquired by Natixis multiplied by the purchase price of €21). Regarding this swap, Air France receives the coupon on the OCEANEs i.e. 2.75% and pays variable interest indexed to Euribor 6 months. At the swap termination, Air France and Natixis will also exchange the difference between the OCEANE price at that date and the initial price of €21;
+ Air France has a termination option on the swap starting December 19, 2012 and expiring on February 1, 2016;
+ the contract is the subject of a guarantee for 100% of the notional of the swap (see Note 24). From April 1, 2012, the guarantee can partially comprise securities provided this portion does not exceed 50% of the notional amount of the swap.

Of the 3,258,150 OCEANEs not purchased by Natixis within the framework of the contractual acquisition procedure, 1,501,475 OCEANEs were reimbursed on April 2, 2012, for an amount of €31 million, following exercice of the repayment option by some holders.

As of December 31, 2013, the debt value amounts to €390 million.

32.2.2 OCEANE issued in 2009

As of June 26, 2009, Air France-KLM issued a bond with an option of conversion and/or exchange for new or existing Air France-KLM shares (OCEANE) with a maturity date fixed at April 1, 2015. 56,016,949 bonds were issued for a total amount of €661 million. Each bond has a nominal value of €11.80. The annual coupon amounts to 4.97%.

The conversion period of these bonds runs from August 6, 2009 to the seventh working day preceding the normal or early reimbursement date.

Since April 1, 2013 Air France-KLM has had the option to impose the cash reimbursement of these bonds by exercising a call if the share price exceeds 130% of the nominal, i.e. €15.34, encouraging OCEANE owners to convert their bonds into Air France-KLM shares.

Upon issue of this convertible debt, Air France-KLM recorded a debt of €556 million, corresponding to the present value of future payments of interest and nominal discounted at the rate of a similar bond without a conversion option. As of December 31, 2013, the debt value amounts to €633 million.

The option value was evaluated by deducting this debt value from the total nominal amount (i.e. €661 million) and was recorded in equity.

32.2.3 OCEANE issued in 2013

On March 28, 2013, Air France-KLM issued 53,398,058 bonds convertible and/or exchangeable for new or existing Air France-KLM shares (OCEANE) with a maturity date fixed at February 15, 2023 for a total nominal amount of €550 million. Each bond has a nominal value of €10.30. The annual coupon amounts to 2.03%.

The conversion period of these bonds runs from May 7, 2013 to the seventh working day preceding the normal or early reimbursement date. The conversion ratio is one share for one bond.

Repayment at par, plus accrued interest, will be possible as of February 15, 2019 at the request of the bond holders. Air France-KLM can impose the cash reimbursement of these bonds by exercising a call from September 28, 2016 if the share price exceeds 130% of nominal, amounting to €13.39, encouraging OCEANE owners to convert their bonds into Air France-KLM shares.

Upon issue of this convertible debt, Air France-KLM recorded a debt of €443 million, corresponding to the present value of future payments of interest and nominal discounted at the rate of a similar bond without a conversion option. As of December 31, 2013, the debt value amounts to €455 million.

The option value was evaluated by deducting this debt value from the total nominal amount (i.e. €550 million) and was recorded in equity.

32.3 Bonds

32.3.1 Bonds issued in 2006 and 2007

On September 2006 and April 2007, the company Air France, a subsidiary of the Air France-KLM Group, issued bonds for a total amount of €750 million, maturing on January 22, 2014 and bearing an annual interest rate of 4.75%.

On July 3, 2013, Air France redeemed a portion of these bonds amounting to €9 million.

32.3.2 Bonds issued in 2009

As of October 27, 2009, Air France-KLM issued bonds for a total amount of €700 million, maturing on October 27, 2016 and bearing an annual interest rate of 6.75%.

32.3.3 Bonds issued in 2012

As of December 14, 2012, Air France-KLM issued bonds for a total amount of €500 million, maturing on January 18, 2018 and bearing an annual interest rate of 6.25%.

32.4 Capital lease commitments

The breakdown of total future minimum lease payments related to capital leases is as follows:

As of December 31, *(In € million)*	2013	2012
Aircraft		
Future minimum lease payments – due dates		
Y+1	637	651
Y+2	612	605
Y+3	549	576
Y+4	526	510
Y+5	469	489
Over 5 years	1,560	1,760
Total	**4,353**	**4,591**
Including:		
◆ Principal	3,893	4,015
◆ Interest	460	576
Buildings		
Future minimum lease payments – due dates		
Y+1	65	58
Y+2	67	59
Y+3	51	59
Y+4	55	44
Y+5	58	49
Over 5 years	288	212
Total	**584**	**481**
Including:		
◆ Principal	426	401
◆ Interest	158	80
Other property, plant and equipment		
Future minimum lease payments – due dates		
Y+1	13	13
Y+2	12	12
Y+3	10	11
Y+4	10	9
Y+5	10	9
Over 5 years	78	87
Total	**133**	**141**
Including:		
◆ Principal	88	91
◆ Interest	45	50

The lease expenses over the period do not include contingent leases. Deposits made on purchase options are presented in Note 24.

32.5 Other debt

Other debt breaks down as follows:

As of December 31 (In € million)	2013	2012
Reservation of ownership clause and mortgage debt	1,321	1,773
Other debt	890	1,066
Total	**2,211**	**2,839**

Other debt corresponds mainly to bank borrowings.

Mortgage debt is a debt secured by a mortgage on an aircraft. The mortgage is filed at the national civil aviation authority (the DGAC in France) in order to be publicly available to third parties. A mortgage grants to the mortgagee a right to enforce the security (by order of a judge), the sale of the asset and a priority claim on the sale proceeds in line with the amount of the loan, the balance reverting to the other creditors.

32.6 Maturity analysis

The financial debt maturities break down as follows:

As of December 31 (In € million)	2013	2012
Maturities in		
Y+1	2,500	1,817
Y+2	1,871	2,256
Y+3	2,095	1,815
Y+4	1,034	2,095
Y+5	1,291	920
Over 5 years	3,491	4,081
Total	**12,282**	**12,984**
Including:		
◆ Principal	10,733	10,999
◆ Interest	1,549	1,985

As of December 31, 2013, the expected financial costs amount to €363 million for the 2014 financial year, €811 million for the financial years 2015 to 2018, and €375 million thereafter.

As of December 31, 2013, it has been considered that the perpetual subordinated loan stocks and the OCEANEs would be reimbursed according to their most probable maturity:

◆ probable exercice date of the issuer call for the perpetual subordinated loans;
◆ second exercice date of the investor put, i.e April 1, 2016, for the majority of the OCEANEs issued in 2005 (see Note 32.2.1);

◆ probable exercice date of the investor put, i.e February 15, 2019, for the majority of the OCEANEs issued in 2013 (see Note 32.2.3);
◆ contractual maturity date for the OCEANE issued in 2009.

Repayable bonds issued in 2006, 2007, 2009 and 2012 will be reimbursed at their contractual maturity date (see Notes 32.2 and 32.3).

32.7 Currency analysis

The breakdown of financial debt by currency after impact of derivative instruments is as follows:

As of December 31 *(In € million)*	2013	2012
Euro	9,131	9,059
US dollar	587	867
Swiss franc	351	357
Yen	664	716
Total	**10,733**	**10,999**

32.8 Credit lines

As of December 31, 2013, the Group had credit lines amounting to €1,806 million, of which only €4 million have been drawn down. The three main credit lines amounted, respectively, to €1,060 million for Air France, €540 million for KLM and €200 million for the holding company Air France-KLM.

On April 4, 2011, Air France renewed its credit facility maturing on April 7, 2013 with a €1,060 million revolving credit facility maturing on April 4, 2016, subject to the following financial covenants based on the Air France Group's consolidated financial statements:

+ EBITDAR must not be lower than two and a half times the net interest charges increased by one third of operating lease payments;
+ tangible and financial assets in the balance sheet, not pledged as collateral, must be at least equal to unsecured financial net debts.

These ratios are calculated every six months based on Air France Group's consolidated financial statements and were respected at December 31, 2013.

KLM's credit facility, which amounts to €540 million with a maturity in 2016, is subject to the company respecting the following financial covenants:

+ EBITDAR must not be lower than two and a half times the sum of net interest charges and one third of operating lease payments;

+ tangible and financial assets in the balance sheet, not pledged as collateral, must be at least equal to unsecured net debts.

These ratios are calculated every six months based on KLM Group's consolidated financial statements and were respected at December 31, 2013.

Air France-KLM's credit facility, with a maturity as of October 4, 2017, amounts to €200 million as of December 31, 2013. It will be reduced by €50 million every year on its October 4 anniversary, and, is subject to respect of the following financial covenants calculated based on the Air France-KLM consolidated financial statements:

+ EBITDAR must be at least equal to one and a half times net interest charges added to one third of operating lease payments;
+ tangible and financial assets in the balance sheet, not pledged as collateral, must be at least equal to unsecured financial net debt.

These ratios are calculated every six months and were respected at December 31, 2013.

Note 33 Other liabilities

As of December 31 *(In € million)*	2013		2012	
	Current	Non current	Current	Non current
Tax liabilities	707	-	502	-
Employee-related liabilities	832	-	844	-
Non current assets' payables	87	-	48	-
Derivative instruments	118	319	85	279
Deferred income	120	6	122	32
Other	468	72	873	73
Total	**2,332**	**397**	**2,474**	**384**

Derivative instruments comprise €88 million of currency hedges on financial debts as of December 31, 2013, including €86 million as non current liability and €2 million as current liability (against €13 million as of December 31, 2012, all non current liability).

Note 34 Financial instruments

34.1 Risk management

Market risk management

Market risk coordination and management is the responsibility of the Risk Management Committee (RMC) which comprises the Chief Executive Officer of Air France-KLM, the Chief Executive Officers of Air France and of KLM, the Chief Financial Officer of Air France-KLM, and the Chief Financial Officers of Air France and of KLM. The RMC meets each quarter to review Group reporting of the risks relating to the fuel price, the principal currency exchange rates, interest rates and carbon quota prices, and to decide on the hedging to be implemented: targets for hedging ratios, the time periods for the respect of these targets and, potentially, the preferred types of hedging instrument. The aim is to reduce the exposure of Air France-KLM to the market fluctuations. The RMC also defines the counterparty-risk policy.

The decisions made by the RMC are implemented by the treasury and fuel purchasing departments within each company. In-house procedures governing risk management prohibit speculation.

The instruments used are swaps, futures and options.

Regular meetings are held between the fuel purchasing and treasury departments of both companies in order to exchange information concerning matters such as hedging instruments used, strategies planned and counterparties.

The treasury management departments of each company circulate information on the level of cash and cash equivalents to their respective executive managements on a daily basis. Every month, a detailed report including, amongst other information, interest rate and currency positions, the portfolio of hedging instruments, a summary of investments and financing by currency and the monitoring of risk by counterparty is transmitted to the executive managements.

The implementation of the policy on fuel hedging is the responsibility of the fuel purchasing departments, which are also in charge of purchasing fuel for physical delivery. A weekly report, enabling the evaluation of the net-hedged fuel cost of the current fiscal year and the two following years, is sent to the executive management. This mainly covers the transactions carried out during the week, the valuation of all the positions, the hedge percentages as well as the breakdown of instruments and the underlyings used, average hedge levels, the resulting net prices and stress scenarii, as well as market commentary. Furthermore, the fuel purchasing department issues a weekly Air France-KLM Group report (known as the GEC Report) which consolidates the figures from the two companies relating to fuel hedging and physical cost.

Lastly, a monthly report, which is submitted to the executive management by the fuel purchasing department, indicates the level of advancement on carbon quota purchases and the forecast related expenditure.

Currency risk

Most of the Group's revenues are generated in euros. However, because of its international activities, the Group incurs a foreign exchange risk. The principal exposure is to the US dollar.

With regard to the US dollar, since expenditure on items such as fuel, operating leases and component costs exceed the level of revenues, the Group is a net buyer. This means that any significant appreciation in the dollar against the euro could result in a negative impact on the Group's activity and financial results.

Conversely, Air France-KLM is a net seller of other currencies, the level of revenues exceeding expenditure. The main exposure concerns the yen and sterling. As a result, any significant decline in these currencies relative to the euro could have a negative effect on the Group's activity and financial results.

In order to reduce its currency exposure, the Group has adopted hedging strategies.

Both companies progressively hedge their net exposure over a rolling 24-month period.

Aircraft are mainly purchased in US dollars, meaning that the Group is highly exposed to a rise in the dollar against the euro for its aeronautics investments. The hedging policy plans the progressive and systematic implementation of hedging between the date of the aircraft order and their delivery date.

The exchange rate risk on the Group's financial debt is limited. At December 31, 2013, 87% of the Group's gross debt, after taking into account derivative instruments, was issued in or converted into euros, thereby markedly reducing the risk of currency fluctuation on the debt. The exposure of the debt to other currencies mainly concerns yen, US dollar and Swiss Franc.

Despite this active hedging policy, all exchange rate risks are not covered, especially in the event of significant variation of currencies in which debts are denominated. The Group and its subsidiaries might then encounter difficulties in managing currency risks, which could have a negative impact on the Group's business and financial results.

Interest rate risk

At both Air France and KLM, most financial debt is contracted in floating-rate instruments in line with market practice. However, given the historically low level of interest rates, Air France and KLM have used swap strategies and options to hedge a significant proportion of their debt. After hedging, the Air France-KLM Group's gross debt contracted at fixed rates represents 69% of the overall total.

Fuel price risk

Risks linked to the jet fuel price are hedged within the framework of a hedging strategy for the whole of the Air France-KLM Group and approved by the executive management. The RMC reconsider the hedging strategy quarterly and can change the hedge percentage or underlyings.

▌ *Main characteristics of the hedge strategy*

◆ *Hedge horizon:* 2 years
◆ *Minimum hedge percentage:*
  ◆ quarter underway: 60% of the volumes consumed,
  ◆ quarter 1 to quarter 3: 60% of the volumes consumed,
  ◆ quarter 4: 50% of the volumes consumed,
  ◆ quarter 5: 40% of the volumes consumed,
  ◆ quarter 6: 30% of the volumes consumed,
  ◆ quarter 7: 20% of the volumes consumed,
  ◆ quarter 8: 10% of the volumes consumed.

◆ *Increment of coverage ratios:* 10% by quarter
◆ *Underlyings:* Brent, Diesel and Jet Fuel
  The strategy of the Group recommends to use three underlying instruments which are Brent, Diesel and Jet Fuel. Currently, the volumes are mainly hegded with Brent given the few attractive prices of Diesel and Jet Fuel.

◆ *Instruments:*
  Swap, call, call spread, three ways, four ways and collar.
◆ *IAS 39 rule:*
  The instruments and underlyings used within the framework of the strategy must be compliant with IAS 39.
◆ *Implementation of monitoring indicators on positions:*
  To ensure more effective monitoring of the marked-to-market positions and a dynamic management of its exposure, the Air France-KLM Group uses the VAR (value at risk) metric to help measure the risk incurred by its portfolio. This monitoring is also reinforced by taking into account the maximum loss and maximum gain which limit the scale of variation of this same portfolio and enable the appropriate reaction.

Risks on carbon credit

To meet its regulatory obligations, the CO_2 emission quota acquisition strategy has been monitored and reviewed during every RMC meeting since October 2011. Its implementation led to the progressive hedging of the requirement for the current year (2013) and to anticipate the needs of the following year (2014), by hedging a portion of the later based on an applicable scope similar to that of 2012.

The European Commission had effectively announced the suspension of the application of its CO_2 emission permit system for intercontinental flights and had maintained its application for intra-European flights in respect of 2012 compliance.

Following the triennial assembly of the ICAO in autumn 2013, the change in applicable scope was also announced by the European Commission for 2013 and the following years. The scope applicable for 2013 compliance should therefore concern intra-European flights. The scope applicable for 2014 still needs to be clearly defined and remains under discussion.

◆ *Underlyings:* EUA quotas
◆ *Instruments:* Forwards, delivery and payment during the quarter preceding the compliance application date.

Investment risks

The cash resources of Air France, KLM and Air France-KLM are currently invested in short term, primarily money market mutual funds and certificates mainly rated A1/P1, the other lines being rated A2/P2.

Lastly, in order to reduce the currency risk on the debt, a portion of KLM's liquid assets is invested in foreign-currency rated as high quality bonds.

Equity risks

The Air France-KLM Group holds a limited number of shares which are listed for trading.

The value of these investments may vary during their period of ownership. These investments are accounted for using either the equity method (associates) if the Group has the ability to exercise significant influence, or at their fair value. If the fair value cannot be determined from a practical point of view, the value of the investment is measured at its acquisition cost.

The Group is exposed to the risk of significant and unexpected change in the fair value of its shares in Amadeus IT Holding. The Group consequently entered into a hedge agreement with Société Générale for approximately one third of its stake (12 million Amadeus shares) via a collar in November 2012, enabling the value of these shares to be protected (see Note 24).

Treasury shares held by Air France-KLM are not deemed to be investments. Furthermore, treasury shares are not deemed to be exposed to risk, since any variation in the value of these shares is only recognized directly in equity when they are sold in the market, with no impact on the net result.

Counterparty risk management

The transactions involving potential counterparty risk are as follows:

+ financial investments;
+ derivative instruments;
+ trade receivables.

Counterparty risk linked to financial investments and derivative instruments is managed by the Risk Management Committee which establishes limits by counterparty, for all instruments except investments in money market funds (OPCVM) for which the counterparty risk is deemed not to be significant. The Group's counterparty-risk reporting is circulated each month to the executive managements, the risk being measured at the fair market value of the various instruments. Any exceeding of a limit immediately results in the implementation of corrective measures,

The counterparty risk linked to derivative instruments is taken into account in the valuation of their market value as described in the Note 4.10.3. Derivative instruments are guided by framework compensation agreements ISDA and FBF. In these agreements, the compensation (in case of default) has to be made by counterparty for all the derivative guided by each agreement,

Counterparty risk relating to trade receivables is limited due to the large number and geographical diversity of the customers comprising the trade receivables portfolio.

The Group has identified the following exposure to counterparty risk:

| | Total exposure in € millions | |
LT Rating (Standards & Poors)	As of December 31, 2013	As of December 31, 2012
AAA	145	104
AA	196	303
A	1,880	1,539
BBB	96	94
Total	**2,317**	**2,040**

Liquidity risk

The liquidity risk is associated to the credit lines held by the Group, as described in Note 32.8.

34.2 Derivative instruments

As of December 31, 2013 the fair value of the Group's derivative instruments and their expected maturities are as follows:

(In € million)		Total	Y+1	Y+2	Y+3	Y+4	Y+5	> Y+5
Commodities derivative instruments	Asset	255	205	50	-	-	-	-
	Liability	(10)	(9)	(1)	-	-	-	-
Interest rate derivative instruments	Asset	14	1	-	1	-	-	12
	Liability	(129)	(4)	(11)	(19)	(14)	(18)	(63)
Currency exchange derivative instruments	Asset	95	61	26	-	2	3	3
	Liability	(182)	(105)	(48)	(8)	(7)	(5)	(9)
OCEANE swap instrument (see Note 32.2.1)	Asset	-	-	-	-	-	-	-
	Liability	(8)	-	-	(8)	-	-	-
Amadeus shares derivative instrument	Asset	-	-	-	-	-	-	-
	Liability	(108)	-	(72)	(36)	-	-	-
Carbon credit derivative instruments	Asset	-	-	-	-	-	-	-
	Liability	-	-	-	-	-	-	-
Total	**Asset**	**364**	**267**	**76**	**1**	**2**	**3**	**15**
	Liability	**(437)**	**(118)**	**(132)**	**(71)**	**(21)**	**(23)**	**(72)**

As of December 31, 2012 the fair value of the Group's derivative instruments and their expected maturities are as follows:

(In € million)		Total	Y+1	Y+2	Y+3	Y+4	Y+5	> Y+5
Commodities derivative instruments	Asset	146	113	33	-	-	-	-
	Liability	(35)	(24)	(11)	-	-	-	-
Interest rate derivative instruments	Asset	24	4	1	-	3	-	16
	Liability	(200)	(7)	(17)	(14)	(19)	(29)	(114)
Currency exchange derivative instruments	Asset	134	84	34	4	-	5	7
	Liability	(105)	(44)	(33)	(11)	(2)	(6)	(9)
Carbon credit derivative instruments	Asset	-	-	-	-	-	-	-
	Liability	(10)	(10)	-	-	-	-	-
OCEANE swap instrument (see Note 32.2.1)	Asset	-	-	-	-	-	-	-
	Liability	(14)	-	-	-	(14)	-	-
Total	**Asset**	**304**	**201**	**68**	**4**	**3**	**5**	**23**
	Liability	**(364)**	**(85)**	**(61)**	**(25)**	**(35)**	**(35)**	**(123)**

The value of the derivatives used by the Group to hedge the Amadeus equity risk does not figure in this table since it is below €1 million.

34.2.1 Commodity risk linked to fuel prices

The Group's commitments on Brent, Diesel and Jet CIF are presented below, at their nominal value:

➤ Year ended December 31, 2013

(In € million)	Nominal	Maturity below 1 year	Maturities between 1 and 5 years					Fair value
			1-2 years	2-3 years	3-4 years	4-5 years	+ 5 years	
Commodity risk (cash flow hedging operating flows)								
Swap	617	617	-	-	-	-	-	38
Options	4,931	3,377	1,554	-	-	-	-	207
Total	**5,548**	**3,994**	**1,554**	**-**	**-**	**-**	**-**	**245**

➤ Year ended December 31, 2012

(In € million)	Nominal	Maturity below 1 year	Maturities between 1 and 5 years					Fair value
			1-2 years	2-3 years	3-4 years	4-5 years	+ 5 years	
Commodity risk (cash flow hedging operating flows)								
Swap	451	224	227	-	-	-	-	16
Options	5,831	4,387	1,444	-	-	-	-	95
Total	**6,282**	**4,611**	**1,671**	**-**	**-**	**-**	**-**	**111**

Fuel hedge sensitivity

The impact on "income before tax" and on "gains/(losses) taken to equity" of a variation in the fair value of the fuel hedges following a +/- USD 10 variation in the price of a barrel of Brent is as follows:

(In € million)	2013		2012	
As of December 31	Increase of USD 10 per barrel of Brent	Decrease of USD 10 per barrel of Brent	Increase of USD 10 per barrel of Brent	Decrease of USD 10 per barrel of Brent
Income before tax	(66)	(187)	123	(194)
Gains / (losses) taken to equity	477	(181)	290	(213)

34.2.2 Exposure to interest rate risk

To manage the interest rate risk on its short and long-term borrowings, the Group uses instruments with the following nominal values:

➤ Year ended December 31, 2013

(In € million)	Nominal	Maturity below 1 year	Maturity between 1 and 5 years					Fair value
			1-2 years	2-3 years	3-4 years	4-5 years	+ 5 years	
Operations qualified as cash flow hedging	**2,272**	**294**	**184**	**461**	**251**	**316**	**766**	**(112)**
Interest rate swaps	1,983	201	154	319	251	292	766	(107)
Options	289	93	30	142	-	24	-	(5)
Operations qualified as fair value hedging	**261**	**28**	**17**	**35**	**-**	**-**	**181**	**1**
Interest rate swaps	261	28	17	35	-	-	181	1
Operations qualified as fair value through profit and loss	**117**	**-**	**-**	**48**	**-**	**-**	**69**	**(4)**
Interest rate swaps	83	-	-	14	-	-	69	(10)
Others	34	-	-	34	-	-	-	6
TOTAL	**2,650**	**322**	**201**	**544**	**251**	**316**	**1,016**	**(115)**

➤ Year ended December 31, 2012

(In € million)	Nominal	Maturity below 1 year	Maturity between 1 and 5 years					Fair value
			1-2 years	2-3 years	3-4 years	4-5 years	+ 5 years	
Operations qualified as cash flow hedging	**2,766**	**146**	**367**	**280**	**244**	**545**	**1,184**	**(155)**
Interest rate swaps	2,307	70	321	182	214	336	1,184	(145)
Options	459	76	46	98	30	209	-	(10)
Operations qualified as fair value hedging	**593**	**-**	**30**	**32**	**60**	**-**	**471**	**(8)**
Interest rate swaps	593	-	30	32	60	-	471	(8)
Operations qualified as fair value through profit and loss	**146**	**-**	**-**	**-**	**-**	**58**	**88**	**(13)**
Interest rate swaps	104	-	-	-	-	16	88	(13)
Others	42	-	-	-	-	42	-	-
TOTAL	**3,505**	**146**	**397**	**312**	**304**	**603**	**1,743**	**(176)**

Based on the hedging operations, the Group's exposure to interest rate risks breaks down as follows:

As of December 31 (In € million)	2013				2012			
	Before hedging		After hedging		Before hedging		After hedging	
	Base	Average interest rate	Base	Average interest rate	Base	Average interest rate	Base	Average interest rate
Fixed-rate financial assets and liabilities								
Fixed-rate financial assets	2,052	2.8%	2,052	2.8%	2,198	2.2%	2,198	2.2%
Fixed-rate financial liabilities	5,965	4.4%	7,486	4.1%	5,673	4.5%	7,752	4.2%
Floating-rate financial assets and liabilities								
Floating-rate financial assets	2,400	0.5%	2,400	0.5%	2,299	1.1%	2,299	1.1%
Floating-rate financial liabilities	4,934	1.7%	3,413	2.1%	5,583	2.2%	3,504	1.9%
Without-rate financial assets	**2,226**	**-**	**2,226**	**-**	**1,521**	**-**	**1,521**	**-**

As of December 31, 2013 and December 31, 2012, without-rate financial assets mainly include cash and the revaluation of Amadeus' shares at their fair value.

Interest rate sensitivity

The Group is exposed to the risk of interest rate variation. A 100 basis point variation (increase or decrease) in interest rates would have an impact of €12 million on the financial income for the year ended December 31, 2013 versus €6 million for the year ended December 31, 2012.

34.2.3 Exposure to exchange rate risk

The nominal amount of futures and swaps linked to exchange rate are detailed below given the nature of the hedging operations:

➤ **Year ended December 31, 2013**

(In € million)	Nominal	Maturity below 1 year	Maturities between 1 and 5 years					Fair value
			1-2 years	2-3 years	3-4 years	4-5 years	+ 5 years	
Exchange risk (cash flow hedging of operating flows)	*4,143*	*2,785*	*1,347*	*11*	*-*	*-*	*-*	*(33)*
Exchange rate options	2,222	1,511	711	-	-	-	-	(15)
Forward purchases	1,509	1,003	495	11	-	-	-	(57)
Forward sales	412	271	141	-	-	-	-	39
Exchange risk (Fair value hedging of flight equipment acquisition)	*1,338*	*429*	*408*	*251*	*120*	*81*	*49*	*(54)*
Forward purchases	1,338	429	408	251	120	81	49	(54)
Exchange risk (trading)	*438*	*72*	*62*	*-*	*98*	*110*	*96*	*-*
Forward purchases	219	36	31	-	49	55	48	3
Forward sales	219	36	31	-	49	55	48	(3)
Total	**5,919**	**3,286**	**1,817**	**262**	**218**	**191**	**145**	**(87)**

➤ **Year ended December 31, 2012**

(In € million)	Nominal	Maturity below 1 year	Maturities between 1 and 5 years					Fair value
			1-2 years	2-3 years	3-4 years	4-5 years	+ 5 years	
Exchange risk (cash flow hedging of operating flows)	*4,414*	*2,949*	*1,460*	*4*	*1*	*-*	*-*	*19*
Exchange rate options	2,278	1,508	770	-	-	-	-	12
Forward purchases	1,717	1,170	542	4	1	-	-	(14)
Forward sales	419	271	148	-	-	-	-	21
Exchange risk (Fair value hedging of flight equipment acquisition)	*1,360*	*471*	*336*	*249*	*105*	*79*	*120*	*10*
Forward purchases	1,322	433	336	249	105	79	120	7
Forward sales	38	38	-	-	-	-	-	3
Exchange risk (trading)	*540*	*82*	*76*	*64*	*-*	*102*	*216*	*-*
Forward purchases	270	41	38	32	-	51	108	14
Forward sales	270	41	38	32	-	51	108	(14)
Total	**6,314**	**3,502**	**1,872**	**317**	**106**	**181**	**336**	**29**

Currency hedge sensitivity

The value in euros of the monetary assets and liabilities is presented below:

As of December 31 (In € million)	Monetary assets		Monetary liabilities	
	2013	**2012**	**2013**	**2012**
US dollar	143	228	519	432
Pound sterling	23	26	-	1
Yen	8	8	727	819
Swiss franc	11	8	341	347

The amount of monetary assets and liabilities disclosed above does not include the effect of the revaluation of assets and liabilities documented in fair value hedge.

The impact on "income before tax" and on "gains/(losses) taken to equity" of a 10% appreciation in foreign currencies relative to the euro is presented below:

As of December 31 (In € million)	US dollar		Pound Sterling		Yen	
	2013	**2012**	**2013**	**2012**	**2013**	**2012**
Income before tax	37	9	(8)	(7)	(70)	(79)
Gains / (losses) taken to equity	312	392	(24)	(22)	(37)	(44)

The impact of the change in fair value of currency derivatives on "income before tax" and on "gains/(losses) taken to equity" of a 10% depreciation in foreign currencies relative to the euro is presented below:

As of December 31 (In € million)	US dollar		Pound Sterling		Yen	
	2013	**2012**	**2013**	**2012**	**2013**	**2012**
Income before tax	(108)	(60)	-	(1)	62	68
Gains / (losses) taken to equity	(220)	(266)	23	22	34	45

34.2.4 Carbon credit risk

As of December 31, 2013, the Group has hedged its future purchases of CO_2 quotas via forward purchase for a nominal of €15 million whose fair value is nil, versus, respectively, €16 million and €(10) million as of December 31, 2012.

These contracts mostly expire within less than 2 years.

34.3 Market value of financial instruments

Market values are estimated for most of the Group's financial instruments using a variety of valuation methods, such as discounted future cash flows. However, the methods and assumptions used to provide the information set out below are theoretical in nature. They bear the following inherent limitations:

+ estimated market values cannot take into consideration the effect of subsequent fluctuations in interest or exchange rates;
+ estimated amounts as of December 31, 2013 and December 31, 2012 are not indicative of gains and/or losses arising upon maturity or in the event of cancellation of a financial instrument.

The application of alternative methods and assumptions may, therefore, have a significant impact on the estimated market values.

The methods used are as follows:

+ *Cash, trade receivables, other receivables, short-term bank facilities, trade payables and other payables:*
  The Group believes that, due to its short-term nature, net book value can be deemed a reasonable approximation of market value.

✦ *Marketable securities, investments and other securities:*
The market value of securities is determined based mainly on the market price or the prices available on other similar securities. Securities classified under "Assets available for sale" are recorded at their stock market value.
Where no comparable exists, the Group uses their book value, which is deemed a reasonable approximation of market value in this instance.

✦ *Borrowings, other financial debts and loans:*
The market value of fixed and floating-rate loans and financial debts is determined based on discounted future cash flows at market interest rates for instruments with similar features.

✦ *Derivative instruments:*
The market value of derivative instruments corresponds to the amounts payable or receivable were the positions to be closed out as of December 31, 2013 and December 31, 2012 calculated using the year-end market rate.

Only the financial assets and liabilities whose fair value differs from their net book value are presented in the following table:

As of December 31 *(In € million)*	2013		2012	
	Net book value	**Estimated market value**	**Net book value**	**Estimated market value**
Financial assets				
Loans	164	167	160	171
Financial liabilities				
Debt measured at amortized cost				
Bonds	3,419	3,788	2,938	3,201
OCEANE 2005	390	428	419	433
OCEANE 2009	633	717	569	718
OCEANE 2013	455	588	-	-
Bond 2006/2007	741	743	750	767
Bond 2009	700	765	700	757
Bond 2012	500	547	500	526
Perpetual subordinated loans	552	248	603	306
Other borrowings and financial debt	1,857	1,770	2,061	1 881

34.4 Valuation methods for financial assets and liabilities at their fair value

The breakdown of the Group's financial assets and liabilities is as follows based on the three classification levels *(see Note 4.10.7):*

As of December 31 *(In € million)*	Level 1		Level 2		Level 3		Total	
	2013	2012	2013	2012	2013	2012	2013	2012
Financial assets available for sale								
Shares	1,100	684	35	20	-	-	1,135	704
Assets at fair value through profit and loss								
Marketable securities and cash secured	31	36	920	920	-	-	951	956
Cash equivalents	1,552	2,653	1,152	148	-	-	2,704	2,801
Derivative instruments asset								
Interest rate derivatives	-	-	14	24	-	-	14	24
Currency exchange derivatives	-	-	95	134	-	-	95	134
Commodity derivatives	-	-	255	146	-	-	255	146

Financial liabilities at fair value comprise the fair value of interest rate, foreign exchange and commodity derivative instruments. These valuations are classified as level 2.

Note 35 Lease commitments

35.1 Capital leases

The debt related to capital leases is detailed in Note 32.

35.2 Operating leases

The minimum future payments on operating leases are as follows:

As of December 31 (In € million)	Minimum lease payments	
	2013	2012
Flight equipment		
Due dates		
Y+1	912	913
Y+2	816	841
Y+3	754	717
Y+4	727	615
Y+5	606	513
Over 5 years	1,872	1,423
Total	**5,687**	**5,022**
Buildings		
Due dates		
Y+1	221	221
Y+2	152	169
Y+3	136	148
Y+4	108	134
Y+5	94	107
Over 5 years	878	956
Total	**1,589**	**1,735**

The Group may sub-lease flight equipment and buildings. The revenue generated by this activity is not significant for the Group.

Note 36 Flight equipment orders

Due dates for commitments in respect of flight equipment orders are as follows:

As of December 31 *(In € million)*	2013	2012
Y+1	381	511
Y+2	436	431
Y+3	616	434
Y+4	536	354
Y+5	931	248
> Y+5	3,828	2,162
Total	**6,728**	**4,140**

These commitments relate to amounts in US dollars, converted into euros at the closing date exchange rate. Furthermore these amounts are hedged.

The number of aircraft under firm order as of December 31, 2013 increased by 21 units compared with December 31, 2012 and stood at 64 aircraft.

The changes are explained by the order for 25 aircraft, the delivery of five aircraft over the period and the conversion of one option into a firm order over the period.

❚ *Long-haul fleet*

Passenger

The Group ordered 25 Airbus A350s.

The Group took delivery of one Airbus A380, one Airbus A330 and one Boeing B777.

Moreover, a Boeing B777 on option has been transformed into firm order.

Cargo

The Group did not take any deliveries.

❚ *Medium-haul fleet*

The Group took delivery of 2 Boeing B737s.

❚ *Regional fleet*

The Group did not take any deliveries.

The Group's commitments concern the following aircraft:

Aircraft type	To be delivered in year	Y+1	Y+2	Y+3	Y+4	Y+5	Beyond Y+5	Total
Long-haul fleet – passenger								
A380	*As of December 31, 2013*	*1*	*-*	*-*	*-*	*2*	*-*	*3*
	As of December 31, 2012	2	2	-	-	-	-	4
A350	*As of December 31, 2013*	*-*	*-*	*-*	*-*	*2*	*23*	*25*
	As of December 31, 2012	-	-	-	-	-	-	-
A330	*As of December 31, 2013*	*-*	*-*	*-*	*-*	*-*	*-*	*-*
	As of December 31, 2012	1	-	-	-	-	-	1
B787	*As of December 31, 2013*	*-*	*-*	*3*	*5*	*3*	*14*	*25*
	As of December 31, 2012	-	-	-	3	3	19	25
B777	*As of December 31, 2013*	*-*	*3*	*2*	*-*	*-*	*-*	*5*
	As of December 31, 2012	1	-	3	1	-	-	5
Medium-haul fleet								
A320	*As of December 31, 2013*	*-*	*-*	*3*	*-*	*-*	*-*	*3*
	As of December 31, 2012	-	-	3	-	-	-	3
B737	*As of December 31, 2013*	*2*	*-*	*-*	*-*	*-*	*-*	*2*
	As of December 31, 2012	2	2	-	-	-	-	4
Regional fleet								
CRJ 1000	*As of December 31, 2013*	*-*	*1*	*-*	*-*	*-*	*-*	*1*
	As of December 31, 2012	-	-	1	-	-	-	1

Note 37 Other commitments

37.1 Commitments made

As of December 31 *(In € million)*	2013	2012
Call on investment securities	3	3
Warranties, sureties and guarantees	288	284
Secured debts	5,756	6,279
Other purchase commitments	155	106

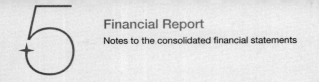

The restrictions and pledges as of December 31, 2013 were as follows:

(In € million)	Starting date of pledge	End of pledge	Amount pledged	NBV of balance sheet entry concerned	Corresponding %
Intangible assets			-	896	-
Tangible assets	March 1999	September 2027	7,022	11,210	62.7%
Other financial assets	November 1999	May 2027	1,824	2,994	60.9%
Total			**8,846**	**15,100**	**-**

37.2 Commitments received

As of December 31 (In € million)	2013	2012
Warranties, sureties and guarantees	135	142

Warranties, sureties and guarantees principally comprise letters of credit from financial institutions.

Note 38 Related parties

38.1 Transactions with the principal executives

As of December 31, 2013, directors and their relatives hold less than 0.01% of the voting rights.

Short term benefits granted to the principal company officers and booked in expenses amounts to €0.6 million as of December 31, 2013 against €0.4 million as of December 31, 2012.

During these two periods, there were no payments of post employment benefits.

Directors' fees paid during the financial year ended December 31, 2013 for attendance of Board meetings during the financial year ended December 31, 2012 amounted to €0.3 million. To join the efforts required under the recovery plan Transform 2015, the directors had decided to give up half of fees concerning the year 2012.

Concerning the financial year ended December 31, 2013, €0.6 million was also paid for attendance of Board meetings.

38.2 Transactions with other related parties

The total amounts of transactions with related parties for the financial years ended December 31, 2013 and December 31, 2012 are as follows:

As of December 31 *(In € million)*	2013	2012
Assets		
Net trade accounts receivable	126	128
Other current assets	25	12
Other non-current assets	7	21
Total	**158**	**161**
Liabilities		
Trade accounts payable	114	183
Other current liabilities	56	66
Other long-term liabilities	72	35
Total	**242**	**284**

As of December 31 *(In € million)*	2013	2012
Net sales	244	215
Landing fees and other rents	(394)	(415)
Other selling expenses	(153)	(158)
Passenger service	(53)	(43)
Other	(49)	(56)
Total	**(405)**	**(457)**

As a part of its normal business, the Group enters into transactions with related parties including transactions with State-owned and governmental entities such as the Defense Ministry, the Paris Airport Authority ("Aéroports de Paris", or "ADP") and the French civil aviation regulator ("DGAC"). Air France-KLM considers that such transactions are concluded on terms equivalent to those on transactions with third parties. The most significant transactions are described below:

▐ Aéroports De Paris (ADP)

✦ land and property rental agreements;
✦ airport and passenger-related fee arrangements.

In addition, ADP collects airport landing fees on behalf of the French State.

Total expenses incurred by the Group in connection with the above-mentioned arrangements amounted to a respective €372 million and €373 million for the periods ended December 31, 2013 and December 31, 2012.

▐ Defense Ministry

Air France-KLM has entered into contracts with the French Defense Ministry concerning the maintenance of aircraft in the French Air Force. The net revenue derived from this activity amounted to €42 million for the year ended December 31, 2013 versus €67 million as of December 31, 2012.

▐ Direction Générale de l'Aviation Civile (DGAC)

This civil aviation regulator is under the authority of the French Ministry of Transport, which manages security and safety in the French air space and at airport. As a result, the DGAC charges fees to Air France-KLM for the use of installations and services which amounted to €105 million as of December 31, 2013 versus €115 million for the year ended December 31, 2012.

▐ Amadeus

For the year ended December 31, 2013, total transactions with Amadeus amounted to an expense of €132 million for the Group, compared with €141 million for the year ended December 31, 2012.

▐ Alitalia

For the year ended December 31, 2013, the amount of transactions realized with Alitalia represents revenues of €81 million for the Group (compared with €53 million for the year ended December 31, 2012) and a cost of €12 million (compared with €14 million for the year ended December 31, 2012).

Note 39 Consolidated statement of cash flow

39.1 Other non-monetary items and impairment

Other non-monetary items and impairment can be analyzed as follows:

As of December 31 (In € million)	Notes	2013	2012 Pro forma
Variation of provisions relating to restructuring plan	11	17	375
Variation of provisions relating to pension and pension assets		(51)	(91)
Variation of provisions relating to goodwill	17	11	173
Impairment of Cityjet VLM Group	14	66	-
Variation of provisions relating to onerous contracts	11	(4)	50
Depreciation of assets available for sale	11	102	-
Other		65	38
Total		**206**	**545**

39.2 Acquisitions of subsidiaries, of shares in non-controlled entities

Net cash disbursements related to the acquisition of subsidiaries and investments in associates were as follows:

As of December 31 (In € million)	2013	2012
Cash disbursement for acquisitions	(33)	(39)
Cash from acquired subsidiaries	6	-
Net cash disbursement	*(27)*	*(39)*

There were no significant acquisitions of subsidiaries and investments for the periods presented.

39.3 Disposal of subsidiaries without loss of control, of owned shares

As of December 31, 2013, no cash proceeds have been recorded on this line.

As of December 31, 2012, the net cash proceeds corresponded to profits of disposal of owned shares for €7 million.

39.4 Non cash transactions

During the financial year ended December 31, 2013, the Group renewed a lease contract for a car park with Aéroport de Paris. This contract is classified as a financial lease.

A lease contract on A340 aircraft, classified as a financial lease in 2012, has also been reclassified as an operational lease.

During the financial year ended December 31, 2012, the Group had entered into a financial lease for the acquisition of an A380 aircraft and for the acquisition of a building dedicated to handling delayed luggage. The Group had also renewed a lease contract for a B747-400 aircraft and reclassified under financial lease the contract on an A340 aircraft.

These operations have no impact on the cash flow statement.

Note 40 Fees of Statutory Auditors

As of 31 December 31 (In € million)	KPMG				
	2013		2012	
	Amount	%	Amount	%
Audit				
Statutory audit, certification, review of stand-alone and consolidated accounts	3.7	88%	3.8	85%
◆ Air France-KLM SA	0.7	-	0.7	-
◆ Consolidated subsidiaries	3.0	-	3.1	-
Other ancillary services and audit services	0.2	5%	0.6	13%
◆ Air France-KLM SA	0.1	-	0.1	-
◆ Consolidated subsidiaries	0.1	-	0.5	-
Sub-total	**3.9**	**93%**	**4.4**	**98%**
Other services				
Legal, tax and corporate	0.3	7%	0.1	2%
Information technology	-	-	-	-
Internal audit	-	-	-	-
Others	-	-	-	-
Total Air France-KLM Group	**4.2**	**100%**	**4.5**	**100%**

As of December 31 (In € million)	Deloitte & Associés				
	2013		2012	
	Amount	%	Amount	%
Audit				
Statutory audit, certification, review of stand-alone and consolidated accounts	3.7	90%	3.8	87%
◆ Air France-KLM SA	0.7	-	0.7	-
◆ Consolidated subsidiaries	3.0	-	3.1	-
Other ancillary services and audit services	0.3	8%	0.5	11%
◆ Air France-KLM SA	0.1	-	0.1	-
◆ Consolidated subsidiaries	0.2	-	0.4	-
Sub-total	**4.0**	**98%**	**4.3**	**98%**
Other services				
Legal, tax and corporate	0.1	2%	0.1	2%
Information technology	-	-	-	-
Internal audit	-	-	-	-
Others	-	-	-	-
Total Air France-KLM Group	**4.1**	**100%**	**4.4**	**100%**

Note 41 Consolidation scope as of December 31, 2013

The scope includes 162 fully-consolidated entities and 41 equity affiliates.

Based on the Air France-KLM ownership in terms of both voting rights and equity interest and on the functioning mode of the Group's Executive Committee, Air France-KLM has the power to manage the KLM Group's financial and operational strategies and controls KLM. As a result, KLM is fully consolidated in Air France-KLM's consolidated financial statements.

41.1 Consolidated entities

Entity	Country	Segment	% interest	% control
AIR FRANCE SA	France	Multisegment	100	100
KONINKLIJKE LUCHTVAART MAATSCHAPPIJ N.V.	Netherlands	Multisegment	99	49
MARTINAIR HOLLAND N.V.	Netherlands	Multisegment	99	49
AIR FRANCE GROUND HANDLING INDIA PVT LTD	India	Passenger	51	51
AIRLINAIR	France	Passenger	100	100
BLUE LINK	France	Passenger	100	100
BLUE LINK INTERNATIONAL	France	Passenger	100	100
BLUELINK INTERNATIONAL AUSTRALIA	Australia	Passenger	100	100
BLUELINK INTERNATIONAL CZ	Czech Rep.	Passenger	100	100
BLUELINK INTERNATIONAL MAURITIUS	Mauritius	Passenger	100	100
BLUE CONNECT	Mauritius	Passenger	70	70
HOP BRIT AIR	France	Passenger	100	100
CITY JET	Ireland	Passenger	100	100
COBALT GROUND SOLUTIONS LIMITED	United Kingdom	Passenger	99	49
CONSTELLATION FINANCE LIMITED	Ireland	Passenger	100	100
CYGNIFIC B.V.	Netherlands	Passenger	99	49
HEATHROW AIRPORT HANDLING LTD	United Kingdom	Passenger	99	49
HOP	France	Passenger	100	100
IAS ASIA INCORPORATED	Philippines	Passenger	99	49
IASA INCORPORATED	Philippines	Passenger	99	49
ICARE	France	Passenger	100	100
INTERNATIONAL AIRLINE SERVICES EUROPE LIMITED	United Kingdom	Passenger	99	49
INTERNATIONAL AIRLINE SERVICES LIMITED	United Kingdom	Passenger	99	49
INTERNATIONAL MARINE AIRLINE SERVICES LIMITED	United Kingdom	Passenger	99	49
INTERNATIONAL AIRLINE SERVICES AMERICAS L.P	United States	Passenger	99	49
KLM CITYHOPPER B.V.	Netherlands	Passenger	99	49
KLM CITYHOPPER UK LTD	United Kingdom	Passenger	99	49
KLM EQUIPMENT SERVICES B.V.	Netherlands	Passenger	99	49
KLM FLIGHT ACADEMY B.V.	Netherlands	Passenger	99	49
LYON MAINTENANCE	France	Passenger	100	100
MILESHOUSE	France	Passenger	100	100

Entity	Country	Segment	% interest	% control
HOP REGIONAL	France	Passenger	100	100
STICHTING STUDENTENHUISVESTING VLIEGVELD EELDE	Netherlands	Passenger	99	49
VLM AIRLINES N.V.	Belgium	Passenger	100	100
BLUE CROWN B.V.	Netherlands	Cargo	99	49
MEXICO CARGO HANDLING	Mexico	Cargo	100	100
SODEXI	France	Cargo	65	65
AEROMAINTENANCE GROUP	United States	Maintenance	100	100
AIR FRANCE INDUSTRIE US	United States	Maintenance	100	100
AIR FRANCE KLM COMPONENT SERVICES CO LTD	Chine	Maintenance	100	100
AIR ORIENT SERVICES	France	Maintenance	100	100
CRMA	France	Maintenance	100	100
EUROPEAN PNEUMATIC COMPONENT OVERHAUL AND REPAIR (EPCOR) B.V.	Netherlands	Maintenance	99	49
KLM E&M MALAYSIA SDN BHD	Malaysia	Maintenance	99	49
KLM UK ENGINEERING LIMITED	United Kingdom	Maintenance	99	49
ACNA	France	Other	98	100
ACSAIR	France	Other	50	51
SERVAIR FORMATION	France	Other	98	100
AFRIQUE CATERING	France	Other	50	51
AIDA	Mauritius	Other	77	77
AIR FRANCE FINANCE	France	Other	100	100
AIR FRANCE FINANCE IRELAND	Ireland	Other	100	100
AIR FRANCE KLM FINANCE	France	Other	100	100
AIRPORT MEDICAL SERVICES B.V.	Netherlands	Other	79	39
AIRPORT MEDICAL SERVICES C.V.	Netherlands	Other	79	39
ALL AFRICA AIRWAYS	Mauritius	Other	80	80
AMSTERDAM SCHIPOL PIJPLEIDING BEHEER B.V.	Netherlands	Other	59	49
AMSTERDAM SCHIPOL PIJPLEIDING C.V.	Netherlands	Other	75	49
BLUE YONDER IX B.V.	Netherlands	Other	99	49
BLUE YONDER X B.V.	Netherlands	Other	99	49
BLUE YONDER XIV B.V.	Netherlands	Other	99	49
BLUE YONDER XV B.V.	Netherlands	Other	99	49
B.V. KANTOORGEBOUW MARTINAIR	Netherlands	Other	99	49
CATERING FDF	France	Other	98	100
CATERING PTP	France	Other	98	100
CELL K16 INSURANCE COMPANY	United Kingdom	Other	99	0
DAKAR CATERING	Senegal	Other	64	65
ETS SCHIPHOL B.V.	Netherlands	Other	99	49
EUROPEAN CATERING SERVICES	United States	Other	98	100

Entity	Country	Segment	% interest	% control
GIE JEAN BART	France	Other	10	10
GIE SERVCENTER	France	Other	98	100
GIE SURCOUF	France	Other	100	100
GUINEENNE DE SERVICES AEROPORTUAIRES S.A.	Guinea	Other	30	60
HEESWIJK HOLDING B.V.	Netherlands	Other	99	49
INTERNATIONALE FINANCIERING EN MANAGEMENT MAATSCHAPPIJ B.V.	Netherlands	Other	99	49
KES AIRPORT EQUIPMENT FUELLING B.V.	Netherlands	Other	99	49
KES AIRPORT EQUIPMENT LEASING B.V.	Netherlands	Other	99	49
KLM AIRL CHARTER B.V.	Netherlands	Other	99	49
KLM CATERING SERVICES SCHIPOL B.V.	Netherlands	Other	99	49
KLM FINANCIAL SERVICES B.V.	Netherlands	Other	99	49
KLM HEALTH SERVICES B.V.	Netherlands	Other	99	49
KLM INTERNATIONAL CHARTER B.V.	Netherlands	Other	99	49
KLM INTERNATIONAL FINANCE COMPANY B.V.	Netherlands	Other	99	49
KLM OLIEMAATSCHAPPIJ B.V.	Netherlands	Other	99	49
KLM UNTERSTUTZUNGSKASSEN GMBH	Germany	Other	99	49
KROONDUIF B.V.	Netherlands	Other	99	49
LYON AIR TRAITEUR	France	Other	98	100
MALI CATERING	Mali	Other	70	99
MARTINAIR AFRICA LTD.	Kenya	Other	99	49
MARTINAIR FAR EAST LTD.	Hong Kong	Other	99	49
MARTINAIR HK LTD.	Hong Kong	Other	99	49
MARTINAIR VESTIGING VLIEGVELD LELYSTAD B.V.	Netherlands	Other	99	49
MARTINIQUE CATERING	France	Other	91	93
MAURITANIE CATERING	Mauritania	Other	25	51
NAS AIRPORT SERVICES LIMITED	Kenya	Other	58	100
O'FIONNAGAIN HOLDING COMPANY LIMITED	Ireland	Other	100	100
ORION-STAETE B.V.	Netherlands	Other	99	49
ORLY AIR TRAITEUR	France	Other	98	100
SERVAIR BURKINA FASO	Burkina Faso	Other	84	86
PARIS AIR CATERING	France	Other	98	100
PASSERELLE CDG	France	Other	64	66
PELICAN	Luxembourg	Other	100	100
PMAIR	France	Other	50	51
PRESTAIR	France	Other	98	100
PYRHELIO-STAETE B.V.	Netherlands	Other	99	49
QUASAR-STAETE B.V.	Netherlands	Other	99	49
RIGEL-STAETE B.V.	Netherlands	Other	99	49

Entity	Country	Segment	% interest	% control
SENCA	Senegal	Other	32	51
SEREP	Senegal	Other	57	59
SERVAIR (Cie d'exploitation des services auxiliaires aériens)	France	Other	98	98
SERVAIR ABIDJAN	Ivory Coast	Other	84	86
SERVAIR CARAIBES	France	Other	98	98
SERVAIR GHANA	Ghana	Other	56	57
SERVAIR RETAIL FORT DE France	France	Other	50	51
SERVAIR SATS	Singapore	Other	50	51
SERVAIR SOLUTION ITALIA S.R.L.	Italy	Other	98	100
SERVANTAGE	France	Other	98	100
SERVASCO	Macao	Other	59	60
SERVAIR SOLUTIONS	France	Other	98	100
SERVAIR GABON	Gabon	Other	54	55
SERVLOGISTIC	France	Other	98	100
SIA AFRIQUE	France	Other	98	98
SIA COMMERCES ET SERVICES	France	Other	98	98
SIA INTERNATIONAL	France	Other	98	98
SIA KENYA HOLDING LIMITED	Kenya	Other	58	59
SIEGA LOGISTICS (PROPRIETARY) PTY	South Africa	Other	99	49
SISALOGISTIC NETHERLANDS B.V.	Netherlands	Other	99	49
SISALOGISTIC U.S. LTD.	United States	Other	99	49
SKYCHEF	Seychelles	Other	54	55
SKYLOGISTIC	France	Other	98	100
SKYLOGISTIQUE AFRIQUE	France	Other	64	66
SOCIETE IMMOBILIERE AEROPORTUAIRE	France	Other	98	100
SOGRI	France	Other	95	97
SORI	France	Other	49	50
SPECIAL MEALS CATERING	France	Other	98	100
SPICA-STAETE B.V.	Netherlands	Other	99	49
STICHTING GARANTIEFONDS KLM LUCHTVAARTSCHOOL	Netherlands	Other	99	49
SVRL@LA REUNION	France	Other	49	50
TAKEOFF 1 LIMITED	Ireland	Other	100	100
TAKEOFF 2 LIMITED	Ireland	Other	100	100
TAKEOFF 3 LIMITED	Ireland	Other	100	100
TAKEOFF 4 LIMITED	Ireland	Other	100	100
TAKEOFF 5 LIMITED	Ireland	Other	100	100
TAKEOFF 6 LIMITED	Ireland	Other	100	100
TAKEOFF 7 LIMITED	Ireland	Other	100	100
TAKEOFF 8 LIMITED	Ireland	Other	100	100

Entity	Country	Segment	% interest	% control
TAKEOFF 9 LIMITED	Ireland	Other	100	100
TAKEOFF 10 LIMITED	Ireland	Other	100	100
TAKEOFF 11 LIMITED	Ireland	Other	100	100
TAKEOFF 12 LIMITED	Ireland	Other	100	100
TAKEOFF 13 LIMITED	Ireland	Other	100	100
TAKEOFF 14 LIMITED	Ireland	Other	100	100
TAKEOFF 15 LIMITED	Ireland	Other	100	100
TAKEOFF 16 LIMITED	Ireland	Other	100	100
TRANSAVIA AIRLINES B.V.	Netherlands	Other	99	49
TRANSAVIA AIRLINES C.V.	Netherlands	Other	99	49
TRANSAVIA AIRLINES LTD.	Bermuda	Other	99	49
TRANSAVIA FINANCE B.V.	Netherlands	Other	99	49
TRANSAVIA FRANCE S.A.S.	France	Other	100	100
TRAVEL INDUSTRY SYSTEMS B.V.	Netherlands	Other	99	49
UILEAG HOLDING COMPANY LIMITED	Ireland	Other	100	100
WEBLOK B.V.	Netherlands	Other	99	49

41.2 Equity affiliates

Entity	Country	Segment	% interest	% control
AIR COTE D'IVOIRE	Ivory Coast	Passenger	20	20
AEROLIS	France	Passenger	50	50
HEATHROW CARGO HANDLING	United Kingdom	Cargo	50	50
SPAIRLINERS	Germany	Maintenance	50	50
AAF SPARES	Ireland	Maintenance	50	50
AEROSTRUCTURES MIDDLE EAST SERVICES	United Arab Emirates	Maintenance	50	50
AEROTECHNIC INDUSTRIES	Morocco	Maintenance	50	50
MAX MRO SERVICE	India	Maintenance	26	26
NEW TSI	United States	Maintenance	50	50
ACAS – ATLAS CATERING AIRLINES SERVICES	Morocco	Other	39	40
AIRCRAFT CAPITAL LTD	United Kingdom	Other	40	40
CITY LOUNGE SERVICES	France	Other	17	35
COTONOU CATERING	Benin	Other	24	49
DOUAL'AIR	Cameroon	Other	25	25
FLYING FOOD CATERING	United States	Other	48	49
FLYNG FOOD JFK	United States	Other	48	49
FLYING FOOD MIAMI	United States	Other	48	49
FLYING FOOD SAN FRANCISCO	United States	Other	48	49

Entity	Country	Segment	% interest	% control
FLYING FOOD SERVICES	United States	Other	48	49
FLYING FOOD SERVICES USA	United States	Other	49	49
GUANGHOU NANLAND CATERING COMPANY	China	Other	24	25
GUEST LOUNGE SERVICES	France	Other	17	35
INTERNATIONAL AEROSPACE MANAGEMENT COMPANY S.C.R.L.	Italy	Other	25	25
KENYA AIRWAYS LIMITED	Kenya	Other	26	27
DUTYFLY SOLUTIONS	France	Other	49	50
DUTYFLY SOLUTIONS ESPAGNE	Spain	Other	49	50
DUTYFLY SOLUTIONS ITALIE	Italy	Other	49	50
LOME CATERING SA	Togo	Other	17	35
MACAU CATERING SERVICES	Macao	Other	17	34
MAINPORT INNOVATION FUND B.V.	Netherlands	Other	25	25
NEWREST SERVAIR UK LTD	United Kingdom	Other	39	40
OVID	France	Other	32	33
PRIORIS	France	Other	33	34
SCHIPHOL LOGISTICS PARK B.V.	Netherlands	Other	45	45
SCHIPHOL LOGISTICS PARK C.V.	Netherlands	Other	52	45
SERVAIR CONGO	Congo	Other	49	50
SERVAIR EUREST	Spain	Other	34	35
SHELTAIR	France	Other	50	50
SKYENERGY B.V.	Netherlands	Other	30	30
SIA MAROC INVEST	Morocco	Other	50	51
TERMINAL ONE GROUP ASSOCIATION	United States	Other	25	25

5.7 Statutory auditors' report on the consolidated financial statements

Year ended December 31, 2013

To the Shareholders,

In compliance with the assignment entrusted by your Annual General Meetings, we hereby report to you, for the year ended December 31, 2013, on:

+ the audit of the accompanying consolidated financial statements of Air France-KLM S.A.;
+ the justification of our assessments;
+ the specific verification required by law.

These consolidated financial statements have been approved by the Board of Directors. Our role is to express an opinion on these financial statements based on our audit.

1. Opinion on the consolidated financial statements

We conducted our audit in accordance with professional standards applicable in France. Those standards require that we plan and perform the audit to obtain reasonable assurance about whether the consolidated financial statements are free of material misstatement. An audit involves performing procedures, using sampling techniques or other methods of selection, to obtain evidence about the amounts and disclosures in the consolidated financial statements. An audit also includes evaluating the appropriateness of accounting policies used and the reasonableness of accounting estimates made, as well as the overall presentation of the consolidated financial statements. We believe that the audit evidence we have obtained is sufficient and appropriate to provide a basis for our audit opinion.

In our opinion, the consolidated financial statements give a true and fair view of the assets and liabilities and of the financial position of the Group as at December 31, 2013 and of the results of its operations for the year then ended in accordance with International Financial Reporting Standards as adopted by the European Union.

Without qualifying our opinion, we draw your attention to the note 2.1 to the consolidated financial statements which sets out the change in accounting policy relating to the application of IAS 19 revised "Employee Benefits" effective as from January 1st, 2013.

2. Justification of assessments

The accounting estimates used in the preparation of the consolidated financial statements were made in a context of an economic downturn raising certain difficulties to apprehend future economic perspectives. These conditions are described in Note 4.2 to the consolidated financial statements. Such is the context in which we made our own assessments that we bring to your attention in accordance with the requirements of Article L. 823-9 of the French Commercial Code (Code de commerce):

+ the company recognized deferred tax assets based on the future taxable income determined based on medium and long term business plans as described in notes 4.2, 4.22 and 13 to the consolidated financial statements. Our procedures consisted in analyzing the data and assumptions used by Air France-KLM's management in order to verify the recoverability of these deferred tax assets;
+ notes 4.2, 4.17 and 31.1 to the consolidated financial statements specify the accounting policies for employee benefits. These benefits and obligations were evaluated by external actuaries. Our procedures consisted in examining the data used, assessing the assumptions made and verifying that the information included in note 31.1 to the consolidated financial statements was appropriate. In addition, we verified that the accounting policy used for the recognition of the pension fund surplus as outlined in Note 4.17 to the consolidated financial statements was appropriate. Lastly, as mentioned in the first part of this report, note 2.1 to the consolidated financial statements describes the change in the accounting policy done this year relating to the accounting of employee benefits. As part of assessment of accounting principles applied by your company, we have verified the correct application of this change in the accounting policy and the information disclosed on it;
+ Air France-KLM's management is required to adopt judgment and estimates concerning determination of the provisions for risk and charges which are described in Notes 3.1, 11, 31.2, 31.3 and 31.4 to the consolidated financial statements. We have examined particularly the estimates and the assumptions used regarding the restructuring provision booked in 2013 and linked to the Transform 2015 plan and the provisions accounted for the anti-trust litigations to which the Company is exposed. We have also verified that the information as disclosed in the notes to the consolidated financial statements was appropriate;
+ notes 4.2, 4.14 and 19 to the consolidated financial statements describe the estimates and assumptions that Air France-KLM's management was required to make regarding the impairment tests of tangible and intangible assets. We have examined the data and assumptions on which these impairment tests were based as well as the procedures for implementing impairment tests, as described in the notes;

✦ Air France-KLM's management is required to make estimates and assumptions relating to the recognition of revenue arising from issued but unused tickets and its Frequent Flyer Program, in accordance with the terms and conditions described in Notes 4.2, 4.6 and 4.7 to the consolidated financial statements. Our procedures consisted in analyzing the data used, assessing the assumptions made and reviewing the calculations performed.

These assessments were made as part of our audit of the consolidated financial statements taken as a whole and therefore contributed to the opinion we formed which is expressed in the first part of this report.

3. Specific procedures

As required by law we have also verified, in accordance with professional standards applicable in France, the information presented in the Group's management report.

We have no matters to report as to its fair presentation and its consistency with the consolidated financial statements.

Paris La Défense and Neuilly-sur-Seine, February 24, 2014

The Statutory Auditors

KPMG Audit

Division of KPMG S.A.

Valérie Besson

Partner

Michel Piette

Partner

Deloitte & Associés

Dominique Jumaucourt

Partner

This is a free translation into English of the statutory auditors' reports on the consolidated financial statements issued in the French language and is provided solely for the convenience of English speaking readers.

The statutory auditors' report includes information specifically required by French law in such report, whether qualified or not. This information is presented below the audit opinion on consolidated financial statements and includes explanatory paragraph discussing the auditors' assessments of certain significant accounting and auditing matters. These assessments were made for the purpose of issuing an audit opinion on the consolidated financial statements taken as a whole and not to provide separate assurance on individual account captions or on information taken outside of the consolidated financial statements.

This report also includes information relating to the specific verification of information given in the Group's management report. This report should be read in conjunction with and construed in accordance with French law and professional auditing standards applicable in France.

This page has been intentionally left blank

Glossaries

Air transport glossary

AEA

Association of European Airlines. Created in 1952, notably by Air France and KLM, the AEA represents the interests of its members within the European Union institutions, the European Civil Aviation Conference and other organizations and associations.

Available seat-kilometers (ASK)

Total number of seats available for the transportation of passengers multiplied by the number of kilometres traveled.

Available ton-kilometers (ATK)

Total number of tons available for the transportation of cargo, multiplied by the number of kilometres traveled.

Biometry

Technique enabling the identity of an individual to be verified, while crossing a national border for example, through the automatic recognition of certain pre-recorded physical characteristics.

Coordinated airport

Airport where a coordinator has been appointed to allocate landing and take off slots according to rules established in advance. All large European Union airports are coordinated.

Cabotage

Airline cabotage is the carriage of air traffic that originates and terminates within the boundaries of a given country by an air carrier of another country.

Capacity

Capacity is measured in available seat-kilometers.

Catering

In-flight catering involves the planning and preparation of meals and the assembly of meal trays destined to be served on board an aircraft.

Code share

In accordance with a code share agreement, two partner airlines offer services on the same aircraft, each under their own brand, their own IATA code and their own flight number. Code sharing may take two forms. In the first case, the two airlines purchase and sell seats to and from each other at an agreed price. The airline which has purchased the seats then markets them under its brand and at its fares. In the second case, under the system known as free flow, the two airlines are allowed to sell all the seats on the flights involved. Each airline retains the revenues generated on the flight it operates and remunerates the other airline for the number of seats the latter has sold on its aircraft.

Combi

Aircraft whose main deck is equipped for the transportation of both passengers and cargo. The freight is stored at the back of the aircraft and is accessed by a specially-fitted cargo door.

Connecting traffic

Traffic between two destinations which are not linked by a direct flight.

DGAC

Direction Générale de l'Aviation Civile. Under the authority of the French Ministry of Transport, the DGAC is in charge of the security of air transport and of air space in France.

DGTL

Directoraat-Generaal Transport en Luchtvaart. Under the authority of the Dutch Ministry of Traffic and Public Works, the DGTL is in charge of the security of air transport and of air space in the Netherlands.

E-services

Range of ground services offered by Air France and KLM to their passengers, based on the new information technologies. E-services notably enable passengers to check in using self-service kiosks or *via* the airlines' websites as well as the use of electronic tickets.

EASA

European Aviation Safety Agency. EASA develops safety and environmental protection expertise in civil aviation in order to assist the European institutions to establish legislation and implement measures regarding aircraft security, organizations and associated staff.

Electronic ticket

All the journey information for one or several passengers which, instead of being printed, is recorded in an airline's IT database, once the reservation has been made and paid for. An electronic or e-ticket replaces a traditional paper ticket.

Equivalent available seat-kilometer (EASK)

Overall measure of production for the Air France-KLM group after conversion of cargo tons into equivalent available seats.

Equivalent revenue passenger-kilometers (ERPK)

Overall measure of the Air France-KLM group's traffic after conversion of cargo tons into equivalent revenue passenger-kilometers.

Fare combinability

System which, on destinations served by both Air France and KLM, enables customers to choose between a journey with an onward flight connection at KLM's Schiphol hub and a journey with an onward flight connection at Air France's Roissy-Charles de Gaulle hub. With fare combinability, customers benefit from a choice of more frequencies *via* one or other of the hubs, for both the inbound and outbound trips. The fare is based on two half return tickets.

FAA

Federal Aviation Administration. Body responsible for civil aviation security in the United States.

Handling

Preparation of the aircraft, involving loading and unloading, as well as the associated logistics such as management and storage of hotel products.

High contribution

Fare classes corresponding to business or first class.

Hub

Term used for a transfer platform where departures and arrivals are scheduled to minimize transit times. Air France-KLM disposes of two of the four major European hubs: Roissy-Charles de Gaulle and Amsterdam-Schiphol. The Air France and KLM hubs are organized into successive waves for arrivals and departures each day in order to increase the transfer opportunities for customers.

IATA

International Air Transport Association. Created in 1945, IATA establishes regulations for the air transport industry and provides its members with a framework for the coordination and proper implementation of tariffs, together with various commercial and financial support services.

IATA year

Financial year which runs from April 1 to March 31 of the following year.

ICAO

The International Civil Aviation Organisation, a UN Specialized Agency, promotes the safe, secure and sustainable development of civil aviation world-wide. It establishes the standards and regulations required to ensure the safety, security, efficiency and continuity of aviation operations as well as the protection of the environment.

Joint-venture

Joint company with two partners, often held equally with 50% each. This type of shareholder structure notably allows the implementation of technological or industrial alliances in order to undertake specific projects common to both partner companies.

Load factor

Revenue passenger-kilometers (RPK) divided by available seat-kilometers (ASK). In the cargo activity this is revenue ton-kilometers (RTK) divided by available ton-kilometers (ATK).

Multi-hub

System linking several hubs, allowing customers to access the networks developed from each hub, thus multiplying the round-trip offer to and from world-wide destinations.

Over-reservation or over-booking

Over-reservation or over-booking consists of accepting more bookings than seats available. Practiced by all airline companies and permitted by European legislation, over-booking enables management of the fact that some passengers cancel their trips but not their reservations. It thus allows many passengers to find a seat on board flights that could have departed with available seats. Airlines usually have a passenger compensation policy.

Point-to-point traffic

Traffic between two airports, excluding passengers prolonging their trip with a connecting flight.

Revenue management

Technique designed to optimize revenue on flights, by constantly seeking a better balance between the load factor and the fares offered.

Revenue passenger-kilometer (RPK)

Total number of paying passengers carried multiplied by the number of kilometers traveled.

Revenue ton-kilometer (RTK)

Total number of tons of paid cargo multiplied by the number of kilometers that this cargo is carried.

Safety and security

Airline safety includes all the measures implemented by air transport professionals aimed at ensuring the reliable operation and maintenance of aircraft.

Airline security involves all the measures taken by air transport professionals to prevent any illicit or malicious act. Air transport is particularly exposed to terrorist acts due to the considerable media impact offered by such activity. Airline security notably includes baggage screening, and the screening and questioning of passengers.

Summer season

Defined by IATA as the period running from the last Saturday in March to the last Saturday in October. The summer season corresponds to a schedule of summer flights over a period of seven months.

Self-service check-in kiosk

Self-service check-in kiosks, available in airport departure halls, allow passengers to check in and print their own boarding cards, without having to go to a check-in counter.

Segment

Section of a flight between two destinations. The number of passengers is calculated by segment carried.

Slot

A slot represents clearance given for a carrier to land at or take off from an airport at a specified time and date.

Sub-fleet

All the aircraft of the same type, with identical technical and commercial characteristics (engines, cabin configuration, etc.).

Ton-kilometers transported

Total number of tons transported multiplied by the number of kilometer covered.

Traffic

Traffic is measured in Revenue Passenger-Kilometers (RPK).

Unit revenue

In the passenger business, corresponds to the revenue for one available seat or for one paying passenger transported over one kilometer. In the cargo business, corresponds to the revenue for one available ton or one ton transported over one kilometer.

Winter season

Defined by IATA as the period running from the first Sunday following the last Saturday in October to the Friday before the last Saturday in March. The winter season corresponds to a schedule of winter flights over five months.

Financial Glossary

Adjusted operating income

Adjusted operating income corresponds to income from current operations increased for the portion of operating leases deemed to be interest charges.

Adjusted operating margin

The adjusted operating margin is the percentage of revenues represented by operating income adjusted for the portion of operating leases (34%) deemed to be financial charges. The adjusted operating margin calculation is detailed in section 5.4, page 159.

Adjusted net debt

Adjusted net debt comprises net debt and the amount resulting from the capitalization of operating leases (7x the annual charge).

ADR

American Depositary Receipt. ADRs are negotiable certificates representing a specific number of shares with a nominal value in dollars. The Air France-KLM level 1 ADR program is traded on the OTCQX Market.

Earnings per share

Net income divided by the average number of shares for the period.

EASK (revenue and cost)

The EASK or equivalent available seat-kilometer is an overall indicator of the Group's air transport activity. Given the weight of the passenger business (including the leisure business), the indicators for the cargo business (ATK and RTK) are converted into the ASK and RPK "equivalents", the indicators used in the passenger business. Unit revenue per EASK corresponds to the revenues generated by the passenger and cargo businesses divided by the number of EASK. Unit cost per EASK corresponds to the net costs divided by the number of EASKs. The calculation of the unit cost per EASK is detailed in section 5.4, page 159.

EBITDA

Earnings before interest, taxation, depreciation and amortization. The calculation method is detailed in section 5.4, page 159.

EBITDAR

Earnings before interest, taxation, depreciation, amortization and operating leases. This metric facilitates comparison between companies with different aircraft financing policies.

Fuel hedging

Financial mechanism aimed at protecting Air France-KLM from the risk of a rise in the fuel price. Involves purchasing financial instruments, mostly in the form of options, whose value fluctuates as a function of the jet fuel price and the related oil products (oil, diesel). The hedging strategy is detailed in section 3.3, page 91.

Gearing ratio

The gearing ratio reflects the respective proportions of Group net debt and stockholders' equity at a given time. This ratio gives a measure of the company's financial independence: the lower it is, the greater the company's room for manoeuvre.

IFRS

International Financial Reporting Standards. International accounting standards used by European Union listed companies to establish their consolidated financial statements. Adopted on January 1, 2005, they allow investors to compare European companies more easily.

ISIN

International Securities Identification Number. Attributed to securities listed for trading on the Euronext market.

Market capitalization

The market capitalization corresponds to the share price multiplied by the number of shares comprising the company's capital.

Net adjusted interest costs

Net interest costs are adjusted for the portion (34%) of operating leases deemed to be financial costs.

Net income, Group share

Corresponds to net income, minus the share reverting to the minority shareholders in fully consolidated subsidiaries.

OCÉANE

Acronym of Obligations Convertibles En Actions Nouvelles ou Existantes or bonds convertible and/or exchangeable into new or existing shares.

OPE

Offre Publique d'Échange. A public exchange offer (PEO) is an offer to purchase shares in a target company in exchange for shares in the company initiating the offer.

Operating income

Operating income is the amount remaining after operating expenses (external expenses, payroll costs, amortization and provisions) have been deducted from revenues. It shows what the company earns from its principal activity before the impact of financial and exceptional items.

ORS

Offre Réservée aux Salariés or offer reserved for employees. Within the context of privatizations, the State sells a tranche of shares to employees of the company at preferential conditions.

Return on capital employed (ROCE)

A measure of the returns that a company is making on the capital employed to ensure its business activity. The calculation is detailed in section 5.4, page 159.

Revenues

Revenues corresponds to the total sales generated by the Air France-KLM group in its three core businesses (passenger, cargo, maintenance) and in its ancillary activities. The revenues from airline operations are recognized on realization of the transportation, net of any potential discounts granted. Consequently, when passenger and cargo tickets are issued, they are recorded in balance sheet liabilities under deferred revenue on ticket sales.

Share capital

Corresponds to the total contributions either financial or in kind made by the shareholders either at the time the company is created or during capital increases. It is equal to the number of shares multiplied by the nominal value of the share.

SSE

Shares-for-Salary Exchange. In connection with the French State's sale of Air France-KLM shares, employees were offered shares in exchange for a salary reduction over a six-year period.

Stockholders' equity

Stockholders' equity represents accounting value of the capital contributed by the shareholders to establish the company or subsequently, or left at the disposal of the company as income not distributed in the form of dividends. Corresponds to total balance sheet assets, net of total debt.

TPI

Titre au Porteur Identifiable or identifiable bearer shares. TPI analysis enables a company to identify its shareholders holding stock in bearer form.